Final Works Media, LLC
8501 Astronaut Blvd
Suite 5, #165
Cape Canaveral, FL 32920

ISBN-13: 978-1449945053
ISBN-10: 1449945058

Visit us on the World Wide Web:
http://www.accusedmadam.com

Blueprint for an Escort Service

by

Vicky Gallas

This book is dedicated to my son, Alex. May he never read it and decide to open an escort service.

Contents

6

Author's Note: *Caveat Emptor*

The translation is "buyer beware" and it's used herein so that the reader understands that owning escort services is not for everyone. Anyone can read this book, but hopefully everyone that does so will not pursue opening an escort service.

I do have regrets from the decade that I was in business in Orlando: First and foremost, I did not start with a complete plan that included a closing date. Other regrets involve specific business-related issues and are discussed in various chapters. I do not regret going into the business as it allowed me to stay at home with my child and earn a good living at the same time.

Tired of living in the cold North or the mid-West? This book uses Miami for its example, and by the time that you're finished reading it, you'll know exactly how to open an escort service in Miami, Los Angeles, Houston, Corpus Christi, Atlanta or any other location. I offer instructions that are easily applied in any city in the U.S., but you could also easily plan it in Miami, relocate in three to four months, and have your money tree waiting for you. More important, every step in this book is stated with a realistic budget in mind – we are opening the escort service on a budget – as most people that consider this venture have little money at the starting gate.

This book is written for those people that suddenly find that they're on the verge of poverty and have the desire, audacity, and guts to dig their way out of that hole. It is also written for the wage slave that wants to live for a change, or the single mother that wants to spend time with her children, not working 50 hours a week for nothing. It could also be for the person with health problems that can't go out and do physical work, or for the bored retiree. The escort business is what you make it, and it certainly can be fun, exciting, and profitable all at the same time. It is a potential solution to financial problems.

Blueprint for an Escort Service is written with legal issues in mind. If you decide to open that escort service, please do so according to plan and operate the business legally – trust me, it is possible and it's how I did it. I made a few mistakes and you have the opportunity to learn from my mistakes. The case against me was created in its entirety, but if I did it according to this blueprint it would not be possible to create a case. The holes in my plan involved my interactions with some of the escorts – trust me on this – one in a hundred is capable of actually being your friend, so just don't go there at all. If opening a service is your plan, this book will save you unimaginable trouble and avert potential disasters at every corner.

My son, when he was six, seven, eight years old, would tell his grandpa that we had a money tree in the backyard. He meant that mommy bought him what he wanted when he wanted it. At the time it was cute, at least to me. Life has changed these days and my grown son has adjusted his lifestyle accordingly. Though spoiling your children is fun when you're doing it, *caveat emptor*. They say that for every year a child is spoiled it takes two years to correct the problem, so use your money wisely. People usually enter the escort business with frugal thoughts, but then the money comes easily and the thoughts are distant memories.

The most important warning that I can state here is to follow the plan. Sure, it will be your plan so it can have some flexibility and that is always a good thing. Your business = your plan. Every successful business venture has a plan though. Please keep that in mind as you embark on this new and exciting adventure in your life.

Several chapters in this book are quite short – we do not intend to reinvent the wheel here and if a topic can be explained simply, there is no need to expand it beyond its realm and complicate it for anyone involved. The entire point of the book is to make opening an escort service anywhere a simple project.

Purchasing this book also entitles you to email me with any specific questions that relate to opening and operating an escort service. I would like to think that I've covered every area necessary for you to create and implement your plan. If you need more assistance than I can provide by answering a few questions in email, I am available for consultations over the phone for an hourly rate payable through PayPal. My email address is at the end of this book.

Chapter One – Defining "Escort Service"

First, and most important, I'd like to define what an escort service is not: In-call operations of any type and form are not escort services and this book does not address in-call operations. Classically, an escort service is a business that sends or dispatches escorts to clients at the client's location. This states it all – an escort service is always outcall and there is never a place for clients to visit. I will add to that by stating that an escort service also never books a client and sends the client to the escort's location. I have encountered such operations, but that's not an escort service and has nothing to do with this plan.

The simple description of an escort service is the telephone dispatch of escorts to clients in the client's hotel room or residence. This book covers each important aspect of the operation, including choosing location, naming your business, setting-up the office, licensing, the telephone operation, advertising, necessary paperwork, finding the right escorts, theft discovery and prevention, setting rates and fees, collecting your money, contracts, credit cards, tax issues, general operation and finally, closing according to plan.

Prostitution is legal only in two areas of the United States. Most people are aware of the existence of brothels in Nevada, but few know that prostitution is legal indoors in Rhode Island. All escort services are not prostitution businesses and all do not promote prostitution. It cannot be denied that there is rampant prostitution in the escort industry in the US, but the blueprint for an escort service discussed in this book promotes the dispatch of sexy escorts by the hour, and not escorts for sex. There is a difference.

Chapter Two – The Plan

Every person entering any type of business should have a plan or an outline of what the business will do, where it will be located and why the specific location is chosen, how it will earn money, the profit margin, future projections, advertising placement, and costs involved on an ongoing basis as well as start-up costs. The business of opening and operating escort services is not much different, although it is easier to create and implement this plan than a plan to open almost any other type of business. The start-up costs in our plan will be budget-minded. You will create your own plan as you read this book.

We have already established what the business will do: It will dispatch sexy escorts to clients as defined in Chapter One. In the example plan, our chosen location is Miami, and Chapter Three explains important issues involved in the choice and how to make your own choice. Chapter Four reveals how to choose names that you will use for your business, why one choice over another, and how to appropriately register those names. I chose *Ariel's*, *Kitty's*, and *Valentine's* for the example business. The topic of Yellow Page advertisements sounds simple, but there is more to it. You could do this without yellow page ads, but you would be eliminating a major portion of the calls, even today. Chapter Five explains types and sizes of ads, wording, costs in our example, how and where to place ads, and why it is necessary if you intend to make money. I'll imagine that hooking-up telephones sounds self-explanatory to you, but it's not necessarily in relation to this type of business. Chapter Six explains what lines to use where and why. Building a presence on the internet is explained, as it pertains to escort services, in Chapter Seven. By the time you are at this point in your project you will have your business set-up in place, and completely legally.

The next step involves banking issues, credit cards, independent contractor agreements, taxes and other business issues, and it is described thoroughly in Chapter Eight. I keep it simple for you. The phone operation requires some attention, and on an ongoing basis. You can't toss it in someone else's hands and party with the money, although you will find help by paying a trusted friend to be your booking agent once you've been in business for a short while, unless there are two of you starting this venture and you do not need any outside assistance at all. You never let the help takeover the business though, so theft detection and prevention is important. Yes, you will encounter a variety of types of thieves in the escort business – from clients to escorts to booking agents. I can help you beat them at their own game sometimes, and other times will advise you to cut your losses. It is important to understand why cutting your loss, and letting it go, is the most intelligent approach when certain situations arise.

I dedicate an entire chapter to the discussion of the escorts, including choosing the right escorts, where to find them, preventing the escorts from stealing the clients and your fees, how they should dress, and general and specific rules that involve the escorts. The escorts represent your business – learn when that matters and when it doesn't. Of course you will need to collect your money, and while this may sound simple and self-explanatory, it's not at all. You must protect yourself and this book is informative as to how and from what.

A main theme of *Blueprints* is about keeping with the plan and why this is so important. By the time you start this escort service you should have guidelines as to how you interact with clients and escorts, and keeping your own guidelines, regardless of what anyone wants, is of the utmost importance. Your plan must also include your second year advertising budget – you don't need to own the biggest service in town and rule as queen or king of Miami, so don't let the money take control and change the idea. When you started this venture, you also set a closing date – just make sure that you keep it, no matter how much you think you need X $s more and one more year is in your best interest. You can always close it completely, take a break – like a vacation – and open a new escort service in a new city far away where no one knows your name. You can do all of that because now you have the knowledge and the experience, or you can move on in life and do something entirely different.

What must be included in your plan?

1. Once you choose the city location for your escort business it is important to set geographical boundaries. For example, in our chosen city of Miami, most escort businesses serve not only Miami, but also Ft. Lauderdale and West Palm Beach, and some send escorts to the upper Keys, like Key Largo. I advise against spreading out this way, especially in your first year of business. Just concentrate on Miami Dade County – the area includes Miami Beach and South Beach. Miami is a highly populated metropolitan area. It's enough to worry about in the first year. If you pick Ft. Lauderdale for your operation, then stick with Broward County. Learn the geographical boundaries of your chosen area. If you want to expand after the first year then do so at that time.

2. Have an idea of the rate range that you want your service to fit. I dedicate an entire chapter to setting the rates and fees, but you should already have an idea of your chosen range. First you must explore by looking at websites in the chosen area and noting the rates advertised. You will also need a yellow page

directory for your city and a man to make calls and ask about rates and services. Get an idea what other agencies say to potential clients. Call everyone in the directory, or close to it anyway. Do you want to be the high-dollar service, the bottom dollar service, or somewhere in-between? It is your decision, but your ads must cater to the type of clients that you want to book, so the range must be a part of the initial plan.

3. How long do you plan to be in business in the chosen city? Pick a date to close and keep it, regardless of outside interferences. For the type of operation described in this book I do not recommend the longevity approach. The idea is to open quickly, make an impact and earn lots of money, and then suddenly disappear. Even with this guide you will still be learning in the first year. Consider the business open during the month that the yellow pages are distributed. The second year begins when the next year books are distributed, and so on.... I advise you to close at the end of the second or third year. Take your time off, vacation, or whatever you want to call it, and if you feel that you did well with this two or three year plan financially, then choose a new location and do it again. I would not advise you to stay in business in the same city for any more than three years. Whether you know it or not, too many people investigate who you are and where you came from – and I am not referring solely to law enforcement – other agency owners want to know where their lost

business went. The escort service business is highly competitive in any populated geographical area.

4. Choose a name for yourself and your partner, if you have one. Of course your real name goes on the paperwork, but when answering the phone you don't want to be known as the owner to anyone – not the escorts, the clients, or anyone. Trust me, it's nothing to brag about and can only serve to cause you problems. The idea here is to achieve the highest level of anonymity possible. Become the persona that you create. I was Laura to everyone except my family.

5. Understand that you do not need to become the escort service king or queen of Miami. Bigger is rarely better in the escort business. Keep it small and attract as little attention as possible.

6. Create your own standards and rules and stick with those rules. You don't need to write them down – I am referring to operating standards. Everyone has their own idea of what is important. For example, you will develop your own answers to any questions that a caller would ask and not alter those answers no matter what anyone says or does. You will also develop answers to any possible statement that an escort could make or question that comes up in the course of business. Your first rule should be to never legally compromise your business or your person – I don't care how well you think you know the escort that makes a legally compromising statement. Hell,

don't even joke about anything that could be perceived as illegal, even if it's not actually illegal at all. I made a statement to an escort that was intended as a joke – it concerned buying toys at *Fairvilla*, an adult superstore in the Orlando area – she repeated the statement in depositions and in trial testimony two years later. Just figure that no one gets a joke that alludes to anything sexual whatsoever, and don't say it. Act stupid even though you're not. If the situation requires it, just hang-up the phone, or if in person, walk away, and do not turn back in either case. **Never reverse a decision to walk away**. Trust your initial instincts.

7. Never let anyone know your plans except the partner that you start out with if you have one. This should be self-explanatory, but I will add a few details here: Escorts and other agencies should know as little as possible about you and where you came from. If you later employ a driver to run errands and collect fees, that driver's paycheck should come from your business checking account, and you can always allude to a mysterious and created owner – you can play the manager. Avoid having any of the escorts meet together – you don't need them getting to know each other as only problems can arise. If you do use a booker that you didn't know when you entered the business, against my advice, that booker should never meet the escorts. Keep everyone away from everyone else and don't answer questions for anyone because you do not need to. Always be willing to walk away.

Tell one person one thing and another person the opposite and it will confuse them if they start to compare notes. Confusion can be good. Learn to be elusive.

Once you finish reading this book, if you decide that you want to do this and open an escort service, you will create your own plan from what you have learned.

Chapter Three – Choosing the Location: City and Office

You do have choices here, and do not necessarily need to choose the city that you live in. For that matter, it's best if you choose a city that you'd like to spend time in, and relocate temporarily to, but not establish a permanent residence in. Don't worry, you won't need relocation money until you're able to pull some money out of this business in order to accomplish the move, and it's a temporary relocation anyway and can be done rather cheaply. I wouldn't want to operate in a city wherein I have a permanent connection, such as relatives, owning property, or growing-up there. That is where I would want to return when I'm finished with this profitable venture.

You will, obviously, need to visit this area several times before you book your first call, so don't pick a city on the other side of the country. The city that you choose should be within a reasonable driving distance. Being in Orlando, I can drive to Dallas in less than a day and night, so in my opinion, this distance is sort of reasonable. Something a little closer would be better, and our example city of Miami is under four hours away for me.

As a part of your plan you should establish a closing date. You never tell anyone this date or your intentions, except of course your partner. One day the service is just closed and the phones turned off. Sorry, but you can't warn the escorts, the clients, or your business acquaintances and new found friends. No one gets warning – got that? Selling the established service is also not an option and you'll understand why by the time you've finished this book. When you close this business, you simply disappear from your chosen city. You tell no one where you are going or where **home** is.

So how do you choose a city?

I am a firm believer that it's not a good idea to open an escort service where you live – I don't care if it's one hour from home, but it shouldn't be in the same city. Now 50 agents will search the country to find my non-existent service – good, let them waste their time. All jokes aside, opening a service in Orlando back in 1992, when I lived in Orlando, was not the way to go. Make it so that you can disconnect from the business if you want to. You will need to set-up a temporary residence in the city that you choose if it's more than an hour drive. This is a business that you must participate in, and if you don't then you will understand why you're not making any money – the booker and the escorts will be stealing it. I live in Orlando and a good choice for me is Miami – this is why it's my example city. It's a 3-4 hour drive, so I can go home if I want to without much trouble. If I did open a service in Miami I wouldn't tell anyone in Orlando. At the same time, I wouldn't tell anyone in Miami that I came from Orlando. Got it?

Choosing the city can require knowledge of legal issues, competition, and money flow, but all of this is easy to research. Let's get started:

Realize that this is not a business that will be up and running in three days, so plan ahead and conduct your due diligence. Realistically, it can be ready to book calls in 3-4 months, depending on when the yellow pages are distributed in the specific city.

Orlando looks like a good choice if you are unaware. There are few escort services here and it's a major convention city. There is no "escort services" category in the yellow page books in the area, but there is an "entertainers-other" category that serves the same purpose. There are plenty of independent escorts that post on websites like *BigDoggie.net, Backpage, Craig's List, The Erotic Review* etc.... There are only four actual escort services with websites. Don't you wonder why? Where did they all go?

The answers are not simple, but legal troubles are like a plague to most all of the disappeared, and also the remaining services. Orlando is one of the most conservative cities in the U.S., and it is the home of Disney World. This is a family town, whether the majority of the people want it that way or not. If they can't scare you out of here, they will simply arrest you, and if there is no case against you, they'll create one. Legal problems aside, as they are far from the only problems in Orlando, there are numerous creative ways to get rid of you here, for example: Your telephone numbers will soon be blocked in area resort PBX systems; some of the better resorts actually have personnel assigned to remove the "entertainers-other" category from yellow page books using a straight-edge razor; soon your website IP address will be blocked by the Internet Service Provider (ISP) that serves all of Disney property, much of Lake Buena Vista (residences and resorts), the Orange County Convention Center, and most of the resorts on International Drive – in other words, the ISP acts as Net Nanny; and they will also do something with wireless service that I haven't pinned down thoroughly enough to talk about yet.

Sure, some of this is illegal as hell, but good luck on proving it. At any rate, this is not the time to start a cat and mouse game with powerful people intent on killing your First Amendment rights – you want a business that actually makes money, right? All of the problems in Orlando translate to few potential clients ever finding your number. Just trust me, and do yourself a favor and pass this city by.

Looking at Miami, the legal issues are few and uncomplicated, and the money flow is excellent. Yes, there is serious competition, but since Arthur Vanmoor left the South Florida escort scene, it is workable. Vanmoor dominated all of South Florida, including Palm Beach, Broward, and Miami-Dade counties for many years. At one point he was arrested on racketeering charges, made a plea deal, and returned to the escort business. He is from the Netherlands and was also deported at one point, I believe in 2005, though he somehow ended-up back in South Florida. He was convicted in 2006 in federal court in relation to a cancer-cure scheme and is forever gone from the escort business. Vanmoor was a creep, and we won't be operating our services anything like he did.

There is competition, but then there is anywhere that could fit our other criteria. We are going to stick with Miami-Dade County and not spread our business out in a three county area. Just choose one county area and concentrate on running the best service in that area. **Bigger is not better in the world of escort services**. (this will be repeated frequently). There are plenty of independents, but clients that choose to call services do so because the independents do not answer their telephone, are unreliable, or have insufficient references and simply appear on the scene. There will always be business for services.

Miami also has great money flow. There are plenty of conventions and conferences booked in the area – research this in your chosen city by checking the area convention center bookings and Google the term "Miami convention 2009" or something similar. The escort business does not count on conventions in Miami though – the area is not a family town; it is an adult playground. Miami also has the port and the flood of traffic that it brings, and it is known as an international tourist destination as well. There has always been a high level of illegal money that flows in Miami also, and this crowd tends to spend more.

Police are not particularly concerned with escort services in Miami, unless of course one stands out in the crowd or there is any type of violent crime or robbery connected to one. Getting a license to operate your escort service is not particularly complicated and will cost under a $100 a year per license with an office location in the county. Anywhere in the county will do, just make sure that the potential location is zoned correctly before you hand someone several months rent and sign a lease. The office will not really be used – you will just use it to check your mail at least once a week and install business lines with *AT&T*. You will use call forwarding – remote activation to send your telephone numbers elsewhere. No one, including any hired booker, will answer in the office, and for this reason the area can be a high crime area – it doesn't matter as long as you can receive mail (don't forward it), install business lines, and buy an occupational license.

One good way to get an idea of a suitable address is to order a copy of the *AT&T Yellow Pages* for Miami. Often the one-line listings will have an address and perhaps you can rent an office in the same location. For a one-room office in Miami-Dade County you can expect to pay between $200 and $500 a month – just avoid the city and stay in the county, as otherwise you will need to be licensed in the city also. Miami-Dade County has numerous cities within, so check it out before signing and paying. *Craig's List* is also a good place to look for cheap office space, and I noted from my own check that I could rent a properly zoned office that's a bit bigger than the broom closet for $250 per month.

Save your receipts on the office rental and for any other expenses thus far. You cannot apply for a license or install a telephone line until you name your business and file the proper state paperwork.

Important Note

If you are seriously considering this venture and are not just reading the book for the heck of it, choose a location city now and use it for your own research as we move along here. Perhaps you will change locations before actually deciding to do this, but at least you will have the benefit of the research.

Chapter Four – Business Names

The first step is to set-up the limited liability company or the corporation, and it doesn't matter what name you give it. Just make the name unique and check to be sure that there is not another corporation with the same name. In this example plan I will use the name "Angel Adventures, Inc." and it will be a Florida corporation. Opening a corporation in Florida is simple and inexpensive. For tax purposes, Delaware and Nevada serve the same purpose. In relation to Florida corporations, a visit to http://www.sunbiz.org explains the simple process thoroughly. This is the Florida Department of State, Division of Corporations website.

If your escort service is in a different state, you can still use a Florida corporation, but must use a "registered agent" – though I recommend you go through a registered agent anyway. Anyone can be your registered agent in Florida – it's best to choose an accountant and then also use the same person as your business accountant. That way all paperwork is kept in one place, but it's not necessary to do it this way, and anyone with a Florida address can be your registered agent. The point of using someone else is that the initial paperwork will have this person's name and address on it. You would be listed on the corporation as "president" or "treasurer" or whatever, but you can use a Post Office box whereas the person that is the registered agent cannot – they must have a physical address. All of this information is available to the public on the Florida Division of Corporations website. You really don't want your office address publicly available to everyone if it can be avoided.

When you form your corporation, make sure that you request the "Certified Copy" and the "Certificate of Status" as you will need these to open the business checking account. For this reason, make sure that you are listed as an officer of the corporation. If you aren't on the corporation paperwork, you can't be on the checking account either.

It is truly best to open the corporation in the state that you will be doing business in. Why cross state lines for any part of this venture? Always avoid crossing state lines in any aspect of your business. This is discussed further in other chapters.

In Florida you also need what the Division of Corporations refers to as "fictitious name" paperwork for any name that you intend to conduct business as. The cost to register a fictitious name is $50 for 5 years, and the name doesn't need to be unique – in other words, ten people can register the same name, but I would advise you to choose a name that is unique in the specific area that you are in business just so that you are not mixed-up with any other company. This is not trademark registration and has nothing to do with trademark. You will not own this name.

When you file the fictitious name paperwork, you do so as Angel Adventures, Inc. doing business as X name, and not you personally doing business under this name. This is important in relation to tax filings (state and federal), a business checking account, licensing, and advertisement.

Now it's time to choose names

For this exercise you need a print yellow pages directory, preferably a major directory in a large city. I'm going to use the *AT&T Yellow Pages* for the Miami area in my example.

Notice that often escort services have names that begin with "A" – look at your phonebook and see what I mean. Any sizable city has a "AAA Escorts" and too many AAAA whatever names, and then the "Abby's," "Accent," "Adrian's," etc.... See the pattern here? First all of the "AAAAA" and then "AAA" and so on are listed, and then "Ab" "Ac" and "Ad" through the entire alphabet. Every agency wants a name beginning with "A". Pass on the "AAA Escorts" – it is too generic, and you want all of your names to be memorable. "Abra-Cadabra Escorts" did work for me.

You will want either two or three names – not one and not five. It's a good idea to use three names and spread them in the alphabet. Use your imagination and choose unforgettable names. For the example business, I'll use "Ariel's," "Kitty's," and "Valentine's" – these selections are in the beginning, middle, and at the end of the alphabet. When a potential client is looking in the yellow pages or in an online directory, your business is viewable wherever his eyes land. Some people skip right over the "A" section because there's too much clutter to the eyes.

So, we are Angel Adventures Inc. doing business as *Ariel's*, *Kitty's*, and *Valentine's*, but read the rest of the book before you register them. In Florida it costs $160 to form a corporation and receive a copy of the certificate of status and the certified copy. Each fictitious name that is registered will cost $50 – the total cost here is $310. Later we will choose one of these names to use for the website, and each name will be listed in the yellow pages and in online directories. Make sure to save all of your receipts.

Chapter Five – Yellow Page Advertisements

The internet is great for many reasons; however, if you're planning to do much business, you will need the yellow pages. Yellow pages are not history – this is where most clients will locate your ad. Pass on this and eliminate most callers. Sad but true. I don't care what anyone tells you.

In Miami the predominant book is the *AT&T Real Yellow Pages*, and there are three books that cover the area – Miami North, Miami South, and Miami Beach. Make sure that your ads will appear in all three directories. The North book looks like it covers the entire area, but simply ask your representative when you place the ads. The Miami area books have an ad placement deadline of around July 1st. The books are published and distributed in October – this is every year. Miami Beach books have a deadline of around September 1st and are published and distributed in December.

There are, no doubt, other companies that publish yellow pages in Miami area, though none come close in distribution. *AT&T* is the one book to place ads in the Miami area. Another top publisher is R.H. Donnelly, but as far as I know it's not published in Miami due to an expensive mishap back in the 1980s.

Every area has one yellow page directory that dominates – it is up to you to find out which publishers are in your chosen location. *Dex Media* is big in the mid-West and Western United States.

Now that you are aware of the main directory in your location and its deadline, we are ready to discuss ad size, cost, and content.

Do not place ads in all of the directories distributed in your location. Choose the established publisher – that is where your ads will be found by potential clients. Once you have conducted the research and know which directory your ad should be placed, contact a representative and order a copy of the currently distributed directory. Some big city libraries also have them, so you could check locally first.

In Miami, the *AT&T* directory will sell display ads in the "escort services" category. In Orlando they do not sell display ads for the alternate category of "entertainers-other". They also sell in-column ads: the 3-inch; 2-inch; 1-inch; ½ inch; and bold print one line ads. Few advertisers in the "escort services" category place ads any larger than dollar bill size, and most are bold print or regular print one-liners. This is an absolute advantage for you because you won't have to compete with full-page color ads or spend the equivalent of a new car to be found in the book. This should also be a consideration when choosing the location city – no one wants to be buried in an oversold book! So make sure that you order a copy of the actual directory for any city that you are seriously considering. It's important to know exactly what is in the book before you make your final decision on location.

In Orlando, back in the 1990s, the *Sprint/R.H. Donnelly Directory* prevailed in almost all of the resorts. In 1996, I spent over $50K on ads in that book. It is now the *Embarq/R.H. Donnelly* book, the "escort services" category was replaced in 1997 with the "entertainers-other" category, and it still has display ads in color. Back in 1996, a three-quarter page color ad cost $3900.00 per month and with a 50% down requirement, starting out would be too expensive to contemplate in our budget plan. This is what I mean by an oversold book.

Okay – back to our Miami ads – I'd recommend the following:

We want some form of an ad for each of our three names, but we are low on cash and especially since *AT&T Yellow Pages* often requires first year advertisers to pay in full for the year for ads, we should go light. If you have great credit *AT&T*, or any other directory publisher, will allow monthly billing. Remember – we also have the internet. You do get a free one-line listing for each business line phone that you turn on, but the freebies do not stand out at all. So we budget.

For *Ariel's* we go with a bold print one-liner in black. We just wanted something in the "A" section, but not much is required. You'll find that most people scan the "A" section with their eyes, though few stop looking at that point.

I would choose a small display ad for *Kitty's*. In that the largest ads that I see in the directory in our category are dollar bill size, I would want a business card size in color. Display ads are sized as business card size, eighth of a page, dollar bill size, quarter page, third page, half page, three-quarter page, and full page. Black and white is sufficient if you have an ad design that fits, but if not, choosing full color will help your ad stand out.

For *Kitty's* we could also choose to buy a 1-inch ad instead of the display ad. The "K" section is half-way through the alphabet, the name is catchy, and we do want potential clients to see the ad. Not too many words can fit in a 1-inch ad, so choose your wording wisely. Most directories have guidelines that don't allow the advertiser to state anything compromising or even flashy, so you are limited in content as well. You could simply put **OPEN 24 HOURS** and **Call a Kitty Girl**, and add **Outcall Only** so that you don't receive 20 calls a day from people looking for an in-call location. Trust me; stupid questions get annoying after a while, and that is the main stupid question that you will hear. People will still call and ask even if your ad screamed "outcall only" – in this case you just respond: "This is outcall only – that's why it's stated in the ad." Sometimes sarcasm helps you to get past the stupid questions that you'll hear so often.

For *Valentine's* we want a bold print one-liner in red. I hope that the reasoning is self-explanatory, but just in case it's not: It will be in the back of the category, we do want it to stand out, and red is a main color associated with Valentine's Day.

One other way to do this in the Miami-Dade County area would be to place your *Kitty's* display ad in only the main area book. You then place the other two bold print ads in each area book, or any variation of this that will get you the best deal possible. The idea here is to spend as little as possible and to have coverage in each area directory in your chosen location. Do not go overboard when purchasing ads or it will cause your monthly expenses to be too high.

It is important to note that advertising representatives for any yellow pages directory have some flexibility; not a lot, though definitely some, when creating ad packages. If you purchase the business card size display ad they can do things like toss in the two bold print ads for free. You must make your own deal – just realize that there is always some flexibility.

The ads that we have chosen will be enough. We are new and our ads will attract callers that are seeking a new service, and we have selected appealing names.

Here is a list of *AT&T Yellow Pages* telephone numbers relevant to this part of the plan:

Sales: 800-479-2977
National Sales: 800-543-1431
Purchase a Directory: 800-848-8000

You can view the actual Directory at:
http://www.realpageslive.com
This is not a substitute for ordering a print directory.

Let's assess our progress:

So far we have chosen the location for our business and composed a list of locations for the office that are acceptable for zoning purposes, come-up with a few memorable names for the services and a unique name for the corporation, and used a registered agent to file the paperwork. We have ordered print copies of area directories and then contacted a yellow pages representative and priced our display and/or in-column ads. We know if monthly billing will be acceptable or if the ads must be paid in full prior to the deadline. Now it's time to hook-up the telephone lines so that we can place the ads in the yellow pages.

Important Note:

Do not go overboard when purchasing ads or it will cause your monthly expenses to be too high. Just don't do it.

Chapter Six – The Telephone Hook-up

I do know that *AT&T* requires a business line that is a landline in any advertisement in their directories. Other publishers may view this differently, but I doubt it so we will proceed on the assumption that this is the requirement. If you are accepted for monthly billing a business landline is always required – that way if you do not pay they can easily disconnect your line.

You will need to have three business lines installed in your office location. List one as *Ariel's*, one as *Kitty's*, and the other as *Valentine's*. Do make sure that the apostrophe "s" is included on your fictitious name filings and also on your business licenses – this is what *AT&T* will request from you to turn on the business lines and allow you to place ads in the yellow page directories. Always make sure that your business names are spelled correctly by every party in each step. This will prevent potential future issues.

As soon as the lines are installed, verify that each works properly. Add various features to each line, and make sure that you include call-forwarding remote activation. You will use this feature to forward your lines to your wireless phone or wherever you want to forward them. Even though you are not yet open, you must be reachable.

Now place the ads before the deadline.

Next you will need to hook-up a couple of cellular phones if you don't already have them. Get two Miami numbers to begin with. You will forward the business lines to one of the numbers for now. The other number will be for escorts to call you for any reason. Do not have the escorts calling the advertised numbers, or the wireless number that they're transferred to, or they will tie your line up all night. Do make sure that you choose the company with the best service and reception in your chosen location. This topic is addressed further in *The Escorts* and *The Phone Operation* chapters.

Let's assess our progress:

So far we have chosen the location, picked the names for the businesses and filed the paperwork through a registered agent, leased an office that's zoned correctly, and obtained our business licenses. We then hooked-up the three business lines and placed the ads through a directory representative, and opened a wireless phone account and turned on two lines. Next we will choose a domain name and create our website.

Chapter Seven – Building an Internet Presence

Once you create the website it will be three to four months before it is high enough in search engine rankings that potential clients will find it. For this reason you must begin work on it now while you await the directory publishing and distribution. It will all come together in four months and your life will change with your income.

First we must choose our domain name. This is very important, so please read this chapter carefully or you could easily end-up lost in cyberspace and no one will ever see your wonderful website. Most people have no clue when they choose the domain name, but you will be far from clueless in this venture.

You must choose a .com – not a .biz, a .net, a .mobi or anything else – just a .com. Figure that the best domains are already taken and you will have to spend a couple of hours playing with this and finding the right domain. You can do this on the *Go Daddy* website. Go to http://www.godaddy.com and search for the domain name. When the name is chosen, you will want to register it as a "private registration" so that the entire world can't see who registered it. Also make sure that you register it in the corporation name, not your name. You can do this through numerous registrars, but just do it in the same place that will host the website, otherwise there could be issues in transferring it that will cost you financially.

I advise you to go through *Go Daddy* as the hosting service is excellent, customer service is available 24/7, and they offer "Website Tonight" if you are on a budget and need to easily design your own website. If your budget is more open, you can have the company designers create your website for you. In either case, your options are always open and they are always reachable – important factors in choosing the registrar and host for your website.

Let's choose the domain:

It is best, if at all possible, to have the city and "escorts" or "escort service" in the name. What ever you do, do not put a hyphen or a symbol or anything weird in the domain name. You do want potential clients to find the website, don't you? Also, do not go on a domain buying frenzy and purchase 20 variations of the name or 20 domain names – I have done it. You only need one so only register one.

Create a list of potential domains and then start checking availability on each. For our example service I checked the following list on July 12, 2009:

1. www.miamiescorts.com – taken
2. www.miamiescortservice.com – taken
3. www.escortsofmiami.com – taken
4. www.escortsinmiami.com – taken
5. www.escortsinmiamibeach.com – taken
6. www.southbeachescorts.com – taken
7. www.escortsinsouthbeach.com – available
8. www.escortsofsouthbeach.com – available
9. www.miamibeachescorts.com – taken
10. www.southbeachescortservice.com – taken
11. www.miamibeachescortservice.com – available
12. www.miamidadeescorts.com – available
13. www.escortsinmiamibeach.com – taken
14. www.escortsofmiamibeach.com – available
15. www.miamidadeescortservice.com – available
16. www.southfloridaescortservice.com – available

This list is just some of the many possible choices. You will need to use your imagination here, but at the same time keep it simple so that clients will remember it if they are unable to bookmark it for one reason or another. I am going to backtrack here for a minute – you can register more than one domain, but only use one for your website. You can always point the others at the one website. You do not need anymore than one, but you might want to purchase a few more just to prevent the competition from registering them, especially if the domain is real close to the one that you intend to use. It's $9.99 or less to just register a domain, and you don't want to bother with any extras for domains purchased for this purpose. A one-year registration is sufficient for any extra domains.

I will confess that I'm tempted to register a couple of these right now, just in case I decide to do this myself, but I'm not – so hurry-up!

For the example business I am going to choose:

www.escortsinsouthbeach.com

I will also register:
www.escortsofsouthbeach.com as an extra so that competitors don't see my website and buy it to interfere with my business.

Yes, people think like this, so get used to it. I like the South Beach theme and intend to use it in the website design. When one thinks of South Beach they picture beautiful ladies from all over the world in skimpy swimsuits, wild nightlife, clubs, neon lights, art deco, fashion, models etc.... This is the type of agency that we are creating.

Now that you have picked your domain name, it's time to decide if this will be a low-budget project or you will hire a professional. Since the example here is to go thrifty, we will proceed by signing-up with *Go Daddy* and using "Website Tonight" to design it ourselves. You can always go professional once you earn the dollars to do so. There are advantages to using "Website Tonight" and doing it yourself, other than the obvious financial advantages: You can make changes whenever you want to; add or remove escort photos, change or add a telephone number etc....

Start by opening an account with *Go Daddy* under your corporation name, using yourself as the contact. After you open the account, call *Go Daddy* to place your order. As with yellow page directory representatives, the sales reps from *Go Daddy* do have a little room on packages and prices. It's not unusual for a rep to knock 10% off the order total. The phones are answered 24/7 and the people at the other end of the line are always friendly. You can get a general idea of your total by choosing from the website and adding as you go along. For this segment of the project, you will spend under $200. You should include the following in your purchase:

1. Register www.escortsinsouthbeach.com for (3) years. Make the registration private. Register www.escortsofsouthbeach.com for (1) year on a normal registration. Just for the hell of it, register www.southfloridaescortservice.com also.

2. Website Tonight Deluxe. This package includes hosting and more disk space, bandwidth, and email accounts then you'll ever use. Pay for 12 months.

This is all that you will need to get your website up and running. Don't let anyone sell you anything else. You will spend about two to three weeks designing your website if you want it to look great and be functional. About half of that time will be spent learning how Website Tonight works. Nothing is too simple.

Spend some time researching other escort services in your location. Google "escort service Miami" and "Miami escorts" and check out the first couple of pages of listed websites. Pay extra attention to the websites with the top search engine rankings – the first page of results – and see what makes those sites work and what you can do to make yours better. Never copy any website, but look at the structure, word placement, and internal page links. Look at this site as an example:

http://www.abbysmiami.com

It's really a simple website with four pages: home; gallery; rates; links. The "links" page is not even necessary – don't use your website to advertise for other businesses, and do not place any of those click-through porn ads, or any other ads, on it. Just use it for what it advertises – your business. Don't state what Abby's states on your website. Your site must be unique to your business. Remember the South Beach theme of beautiful ladies in skimpy swimwear, nightlife, clubs, and neon? You are looking for a "sexy escorts by the hour" theme that involves South Beach. Create something from that.

The search results on Google actually returns few websites when you look closely. Several on the first page of results are for the same business: Elite Miami Escorts and VIP Miami Escort Service. If you do your research, you'll see that these people have quite a few domain names. Not to worry as they charge from $600 - $1000 per hour. We will get to the rates and fees for our project service in a later chapter, but this outfit will not be your competition.

When you start to design the website, always remember to keep it simple. Potential clients should see the telephone number on each page, on top and bottom, and do not put the telephone number in a banner or a photo because the search engine robots will not pick it up if you do. You do not need to link each photo to the escort's bio, and instead just offer a short description of the escort under the photo. Clients don't really care about any more than the basic stats and the photo, and in our business we are only serving one area: Miami-Dade, including South Beach and Miami Beach, so stating where an escort travels is immaterial. You will state the areas that you serve on the main page. Our service will have one rate that is the same for each escort, so there's no need for a rate description on the escort's bio either.

Just remember that potential clients rarely read through much of anything. Few even bother to click on the "rates" page; instead they call and ask. You do need to have nice and accurate photos of real escorts, but NO PORN. Just keep it sexy, not implying that there is sex for sale. You must understand the difference between sending out escorts for sex and sending out sexy escorts. That should be your motto with this business: **We send out sexy escorts by the hour. The escorts are paid for their time and company.**

Consider that your website should consist of only three or four pages: The Escorts; Rates; and Home. On the "home" page, you will offer a basic description of where you serve, the hours that the business is open, and the services offered. Use pertinent keywords splattered throughout the page, and make the telephone number a large font size. It must stand out. Also place an email button on each page. To design your own buttons and banners, go to the *Cool Text Graphics Generator* website: http://cooltext.com . It's free and you can play with designs all day if you want to. When you save your creations, save as miamiescorts1.jpg, escortservicebanner1.jpg, miamiescortsmichelle.jpg etc…. Search engine robots do pick up on file names.

You might want to put a short disclaimer on the main page of your website. There are examples on most escort service websites on the internet, but here is one that I like more than the others. Scroll to the bottom of the page to read it:

www.abbysmiami.com

Keep working on the website until it looks great. Play with it and fine tune it. Of course you won't have any photos of escorts to begin with, but that's okay as you will in short time. Make sure that you state "always hiring" on the website to encourage interested escorts to contact you. Now, time to move on to other internet advertising.

Your website on the internet

Once you have finished your website, except for the photos, you will need to open a Google account. You will use this account for a variety of purposes. To start with, you need to list your business with Google Maps. When a person uses keywords, for example "Miami escorts" or "escort service Miami" or any arrangement of these words, including "south beach escorts" and "escort service south beach," your free Google Maps listing will be on the side of the map on the top of the page. Google Maps will verify you by phone if you choose this option, and it's much quicker than the verification by mail. Use a nearby address though – do not use your business address as it could be dangerous for anyone to know where your office is.

Next you will repeat this process on MSN Maps so that your business will be listed next to the top on Bing. Yahoo Maps retrieves listings from other listing services on the internet, so start by signing-up with the other directories. There are many, though the most important are:

www.magicyellow.com
www.localsearch.com
www.yellowpages.com
www.local.com
www.superpages.com

Your main keywords are always "escort service" and the location is Miami. All of the listing services noted offer free listings. Just apply this to the city of your choice.

Now you must submit your website to Google, Yahoo, and Bing:

www.google.com/addurl
http://search.yahoo.com/info/submit.html
www.bing.com/docs/submit.aspx

Google Maps: Important Information

I have been experimenting with submitting to Google Maps and figured out that once your listing is submitted and verified by phone, you can only delete or suspend the listing by mail. They mail you a post-card with a PIN to the address in the listing. This would be okay, except that we decided to make up an address for safety reasons. So, before submitting the listing, consider that it's probably going to be there for a long time. Additionally, if other directories that Google receives listings from pick up on your listing it is close to impossible to delete it. Just be sure that you want it – don't fool around with it as I have.

Important Notes

Do not submit your website to 100 other search engines for $19.99 or allow any service to submit to the top three search engines. You only need to submit to these three. In short time your website will be in most of the rest of the search engines as most gain listings from the top three.

You are truly finished except to check these search engines on occasion and make sure that your website is listed. If you do all of this correctly, your site will be on the first page of listings within 3 to 4 months. In the beginning, you should submit the website every week, but as you see the website move up in rank, just submit it once a month to each search engine.

I advise you not to set appointments through email. When responding to email, offer only basic information. Include a link to the website (they may have found your email address through a directory), and your telephone number. Instruct the emailer to call you if interested in an appointment. During my last year in business I made the mistake of believing that a client that emailed an appointment request was really a client – it was an agent pretending to be the repeat client. There is more on this story in my other book. It is easier to deceive in email than when having an actual conversation on the phone.

I have never been into texting, though I know many people that are. I always ignore text messages to a business number – I might dial the person back to speak with them, but I'd never text back. You never know who you're actually having a text conversation with, and there's a record of every word somewhere. Always know who specifically you are exchanging words with in this business – the only way to do that is to have a voice conversation.

Let's check our progress:

We have purchased the domain name(s) and Website Tonight to design our website and host it. We submitted listing information to each directory and then submitted our URL to the main three search engines and signed-up for Google Maps and MSN Maps. In so far as internet advertising is concerned, we are done except for a listing check and submission as directed. We will later add photos of escorts that are actually available for appointments.

Chapter Eight – Banking Stuff and Business Matters

Get a federal tax ID for your corporation. This is called an EIN (Employer Identification Number) and can be done on the IRS website or by calling (800)829-4933. If you call the toll-free number they will ask some questions and give you the EIN immediately. You need the EIN to open your business bank account. An international applicant must call (215)516-6999.

Now that you have your EIN, open a business checking account. Hopefully you already know how to do this. You will need your federal tax ID and your Certificate of Status and certified document that you received from the state when you filed the corporation paperwork.

If you haven't already ordered business cards, do it now. Get a box of 1000. Use the business name of your choice on the cards, but underneath the name write "A Destination Management Company" – that way there is not an immediate problem if the wrong person finds the card. Keep the card simple and make sure the telephone number that correlates to the correct business name is on the card. I wouldn't place the website address on the card.

Let's discuss credit cards for a minute (that's all it will take):

Do not accept credit cards or any form of payment other than cash. This escort service will only accept cash. Why? Well, because any other form of payment becomes a solid connection between you and the client. This connection creates a client list for the bank and the government. Your clients are entitled to privacy whether they want it or not. Only an idiot wants to pay an escort service with a credit card, and yes, there are plenty of idiots out there, but you will not be helping them. I do not care how legal anyone tells you it is to accept credit cards, because it is legal. That is not the point. Disregard this paragraph and don't complain to me when you are arrested and/or indicted, because I don't want to hear it. Don't let greed get the best of you. Trust me; there are plenty of cash machines all over the place.

You will need an accountant, but not yet. The checks that you write on the business checking account will serve as record of expenses, so just use the business account for business expenses. For any accounting related questions, ask an accountant; however, make it clear to the accountant how your business works. I have seen escort service owners do this in a variety of ways, but this is how I did it for 10 years:

The money that you make in fees is deposited in your business checking account. The business expenses and monthly bills are paid with business checks if it's possible – sometimes it's not. The escorts are independent contractors and they will be paying you a fee for services, and the service that you provide is that of a referral agent or booking agent. No escort will ever be an employee and the rest of this book is based on this premise. Your business checking account and your receipts will be a record of your corporation's income and expenses.

Once the money earned from fees is beyond all expenses, you will start writing yourself a regular paycheck – or you could just write a check when you need or want to remove money from the account, but either way, you are the employee. You may hire another employee at a later date and will then write them a paycheck. Never pay an employee in cash. An example of an employee would be a driver that collects your fees and runs errands for you, or the employee could also be your partner in this venture. Booking agents can also be independent contractors if you create a contract with the person and send the booker a 1099 at the end of the year. Before you call a booking agent an independent contractor, visit the IRS website and read the differences between **employee** and **independent contractor** – there are distinct differences. Once you start writing yourself, or anyone else, a paycheck, it will be necessary to see the accountant of your choice each quarter – every three months.

An escort working with your agency can never be considered an employee. The main reason for this is that you do not pay the escort, and the escort pays you. You have no way of knowing how much an escort collects. Done correctly, an escort should be mailing your corporation a 1099 at the end of the year. For all you know, the escort could be collecting half of the fee that you quote the customer, or double the fee quoted on the telephone. Only the escort knows what she collects

There are many other reasons that an escort cannot be an employee, so never treat an escort as an employee. Never require an escort to work specific hours or days: just require the escort to give you her/his schedule, preferably on a weekly basis. You must have some idea when the escorts will be available, but you never dictate that an escort must be available. We will tackle this in-depth in the chapter "The Escorts" so this is just the basics.

You must have an agreement with an independent contractor. This is a sample agreement, and it always worked for me; however, if you want a perfect agreement contract, go to an attorney and pay for one. Really a contract is as good as what it states and this one covers your business in a variety of ways, but if you state something to someone that contradicts your own contract, do not expect the contract to save you from legal problems.

I usually required the escorts to have the contract notarized – as I sat in trial this certainly helped in my defense – as it is undeniably an agreement. If I had not required the escorts to have it notarized, perhaps denial of a signature would have been possible. Who knows, but I'm glad I didn't have to find out the hard way. For all intended purposes, you writing the escort's driver's license number, expiration date, date of birth, and verifying her signature with the driver's license signature should be just as good as having the contract notarized. Just look closely at the driver's license – notaries are skilled in this respect. Do not forget to copy the agreement after the escort signs and provide the escort with a copy later. Feel free to add any stipulation that is important to you to this example agreement.

The independent contractor agreement that worked for me:

Independent contractor Agreement

This agreement is made on this _____ day of _____, 2009 by and between _____, hereinafter referred to as AGENCY, and _____, hereinafter referred to as CONTRACTOR. The purpose of this agreement is for the AGENCY to contract the services of the independent CONTRACTOR and to outline the important points in the mutual relationship of both. As the CONTRACTOR I agree to the following ____ provisions in a total of _____ page(s):

1. I do understand that I am not an employee of the AGENCY and I am an independent contractor. It is my responsibility to obtain any license necessary and pay any taxes for income earned as a CONTRACTOR of the AGENCY.

2. As the CONTRACTOR it is my responsibility to provide the AGENCY with a schedule of availability. The AGENCY does not schedule the CONTRACTOR for specific days and hours.

3. I understand that the AGENCY can and will immediately terminate this agreement should it be brought to the attention of an AGENCY representative that I have accepted money, or any type of pay-

ment whatsoever, for sexual or prostitution services
as defined by the State of _____ Statutes.
I understand that the AGENCY is a referral service
only. In exchange for an advertising and scheduling
commission from its CONTRACTORS, the
AGENCY facilitates introductions of consenting
adults for the sole purpose of companionship.

4. The AGENCY, _____,
may do business under a variety of fictitious names. I
understand that this agreement applies to the
AGENCY and any of its legal fictitious names.

5. I understand that the clients referred by the
AGENCY are entitled to their individual privacy. As
a CONTRACTOR of the AGENCY I agree to abide
by the AGENCY policy of absolute privacy. I understand the AGENCY gives its clients a guarantee of
absolute privacy. I will not give anyone a client's
name, address, or telephone number, or any information whatsoever about him/her to any other party.

6. I agree not to violate the laws of the State of
_____, any U.S. Codes, or any local
ordinances during the course of my contracted work
for the AGENCY. This is further defined as while I
am on-call or available for an AGENCY referral or
actually in an appointment in which the AGENCY
has referred me.

7. This agreement may be cancelled verbally at any time by either AGENCY or CONTRACTOR. Regardless of cancellation by either party, I understand that I am still obligated under provision #5.

_____
Independent Contractor

_____
Date

_____
Agency Representative

_____
Date

_____

_____

Chapter Nine – Setting Rates and Fees

We do not want to compete with the $600-1000 an hour service that we uncovered in our research. We also do not want to be the bottom dollar escort service. Do not misunderstand me – cheap escort services do make money, and probably more money than our service will; however, it isn't worth dealing with the many trashy people that you will encounter on a regular basis. In this plan we only send out escorts that have class and know how to dress appropriately. By now I am assuming that you have researched most agencies in the yellow pages and are aware of the range of rates.

If our service is in Miami it would be intelligent to charge $400 per hour or two hours for $700. This would place our agency in the high-end of the middle of the range of rates.

You should not set different rates for the escorts, although at some point you might consider having a **feature escort**, as some potential clients will call and request the best escort that you have available. Of course the best will be a higher rate per hour and a two-hour minimum. A feature escort is not much different than a feature entertainer in the men's clubs. This would be an exceptionally beautiful, intelligent, and personable escort that you will feature on the website. Create a page on your website for "feature escort" and post several photos and a lengthier bio. The rate will be higher for this escort, perhaps $500 or more per hour with a minimum number of hours (usually 2 hours). The escort must understand the rate and the split and be in agreement with it. You will post her availability hours and days, and request as much advance notice as is possible from interested clients.

The rates that you quote on the website or on the telephone will always have some flexibility, if you want them to. In other words, if too many callers hear the rate, say thank-you, and hang-up the phone, you may want to adjust the rate for the time being. On the other hand, if you are swamped with calls and are backed-up, it would be time to raise the rate a bit. Hopefully you get the idea here: You do not want every escort with three clients waiting for her, but you do not want that escort bored and seeking work elsewhere either. Make it clear to each escort that you interview that you will adjust rates when you need to, and apprise each escort of the agency fee that you expect for a variety of rates. Always inform the escort of the rate and agency fee when you give her the information. This way there is never a dispute about a fee later.

The most important thing to remember in relation to setting the rates and quoting rates on the phone is that there is always flexibility. You can offer repeat clients a break in the rate as well; that way you keep them calling you. Although I state that there should be flexibility, realize that we all have our low-end price: you will for the agency fee and the escort will for her money. Don't let cheap clients turn your business into a bottom-dollar escort service. Sometimes it's better to let a client dial elsewhere and find out that the competition with the lower rates has problematic escorts or escorts on drugs etc.... Every client is not necessarily a good client. With an escort agency, the client is not always right. Do not forget that you work with the escort on a regular basis, and not necessarily the client.

The rate that you quote will decide the type of client that uses your agency. If you booked calls in Miami at $200 for one hour, you will book a lot more calls, but then you must have escorts that are willing to go out for $100-120, and this will not be simple. You'll find the escorts, but it will be cat and mouse games all night collecting your money. Most will dress like they shop at *Walmart*, they won't have a clue how to speak to clients on the phone, and many will be on drugs. If you're up to all of this, then go for the volume of calls and chase everyone all night! It is up to you. You will make more money doing it this way if you have the stamina to deal with it.

One other viable option is to separate the services – the lines are already separated – and have your main service that includes two telephone lines and the website at one price ($350-400) and the other lone line as a lower-priced service that charges $200 or somewhere close to it. The good news is that you could use the escorts that work for the lower-priced service for the higher-priced service if it was necessary, though the clients would probably never call you again. The options are limited only by your imagination and how much you can deal with.

Agency Fees and Splits

Most escort agencies take 50% of the quoted rate as a fee, but we aren't going to do that with our agency. If the escort perceives that you are gouging on fees, she will steal the clients and see them without paying you any fee. Of course you'll know this in short time, but why start it to begin with? Some will see the clients on their own no matter what fee you take, but by the time you're finished with the book you will have a solid idea of how to catch this and stop it in its tracks.

There are many reasons for charging escorts exorbitant fees. The brothels in Nevada take 50% of everything, including tips, and likely do this with the preconceived notion that everyone will steal. This is usually a correct assumption. Be mindful that if you decide on this strategy you will participate in encouraging the few honest escorts that you encounter to join the thieves and pass out their telephone numbers.

If taking 50% is a consideration then I would advise that you reward for honesty. Within a month or two after a new escort starts working with your agency you will know if she's honest or not. Often it doesn't even take a month to know where you stand, and of course you can also test honesty, but this was something that I didn't waste time and money doing, mainly because an escort that is honest today can be a thief tomorrow. You are dealing with people and situations always evolve.

For the 10 years that I operated services in Orlando, I took one-third of what I quoted, or as close to that figure as possible. In a sense, my fees were too low. For our example business I am going to suggest the following, if you quote:

$500 for one hour – agency fee of $200
$450 for one hour – agency fee of $180
$400 for one hour – agency fee of $160
$350 for one hour – agency fee of $140
$300 for one hour – agency fee of $120

If you quote less than $300 for one hour you should still take a $100 fee, but the better escorts will not be likely to work at the lower prices. If you decide that an escort is honest, and not passing out her telephone number, consider knocking $20 off of your fee.

Regardless of the rates and fees that you choose to work with, just make sure that you keep track of who owes what amount or you will lose in the ensuing confusion.

Theft prevention and control will be discussed in the next three chapters as it pertains to the escorts, the phone operation, and collecting your money. I have caught many escorts over the years and several booking agents, and I often changed how I dealt with it. I will give you discovery strategies and options to deal with the problem – believe it or not, escort business owners do not usually cut-off escorts that are thieves, though sometimes that is the best way to go.

Chapter Ten – The Phone Operation

There are choices in relation to how the phone operation is run, and as with any plan, you should have a general idea of your intentions before you get started. I am not a fan of landlines, and I appreciate the freedom of wireless service, so in our example business that's the direction I'm headed. Besides, we already have three business landlines in our empty office, and all three have call-forwarding remote activation. These lines can be easily forwarded to any line that you choose: to your sister's line in Indiana or to your cellular phone. We do not need landlines installed in the home.

The first step with this is to be sure that you have signed-up with the wireless company with the best service and reception in the Miami area. There is nothing like service that cuts out frequently or too many dropped calls. I won't name the bad companies, but I will tell you that *Sprint PCS* has always worked for me in Florida. Reception all over Miami is great. Just check it out before you sign on the dotted line.

If you think like me and have no interest in additional landlines, you will probably want three wireless phones for this operation: one to forward your main business lines to (the line with the better ad in the yellow pages and the website number); one to forward the other, lower-priced agency, landline to; and one for the escorts to call on. Of course you will want to make sure that the number on the website matches the line in which you quote the same price.

Here is how I would do it:

The *Kitty's* line with the small display ad in the yellow pages is matched with the website and forwarded to wireless phone #1. The *Valentine's* line is also forwarded to wireless phone #1. This is the higher priced service at $350 to $400 for one hour.

The *Ariel's* line is forwarded to wireless phone #2. If you decided to separate the prices, this will be the lower-priced agency.

Wireless phone #3 will be used exclusively by the escorts. Each will be given this number as the call-in number for any reason. The escorts should be told to never call you on any other line.

In so far as mixing the lines goes, any variation of the above arrangement will work – just be sure that you have the number on the website matched with the line that you quote the higher rate. Trust me;

you do not want to quote low rates on the website. The only bills for this set-up will be your wireless services bill and the business line bill for all three lines.

Who answers the telephones?

The short answer to the question is that you do. This is a hands-on operation. You cannot hand it over to someone else and expect to make much money. You should have a trusted friend or relative that also needs money and is willing to answer on occasion, or on a regular schedule, so that you have some time to yourself. You do not want to hire a booking agent that you do not trust implicitly during the first year because you are learning yourself and wouldn't be able to properly control your own business. Since it's not your goal to become the escort king or queen of Miami, you will be able to handle it with only part-time help from a trusted person in your life.

If you have a relative in Chicago answering the business lines that you forward, then you must also forward the wireless line that the escorts call. The relative in Chicago must have two or three separate lines – preferably three as that way #1 gets the higher-priced services and the website, #2 gets the lower-priced service, and #3 gets the escorts' line. If this is not possible you can forward all lines to the phones available and the person in Chicago will simply quote the higher rate. Warn the escorts that when the other operator is answering they will be called from the specific wireless number that your operator will dial out on. You can easily add a fourth wireless number to your account and mail the phone to your other operator. Your other operator would turn-off that phone when not answering your lines.

If there are two people planning to open and run this service together this is all hypothetical and you just cover it completely between the two of you. This entire idea and plan works much better with two people anyway.

One important point is that the more hours your lines are answered, the more money you make. Hopefully this is obvious to you. Our chosen location of Miami is a late city – your potential clients are probably late people, so it does little good to answer the lines from 9AM until 11PM. If you can cover the lines 24/7 you are much better off and will earn the maximum possible from this business. If you must choose hours, make sure that 5PM until 3AM is covered. There are loads of calls at 4, 5, and 6AM though. Sometimes the daytime hours will seem useless, but often you will hear from potential clients inquiring about later appointments, and on occasion you will book calls. This makes it easy to run errands and accomplish what you must and answer the phones at the same time. Do some more research and find out how late the competition stays open. In Miami most services are 24/7 and the phones are always answered.

It doesn't matter at all if the phones are answered by a man or a woman. I used to believe that a female voice booked more calls, but later realized that this is incorrect. The booking agent must be able to establish a rapport with clients, with the clients remembering his/her name. Before the end of the first contact with a potential client the booking agent should state their name and personalize the entire process. This way a client will feel that if there is an issue or problem, there is a real person with a name to call, and they'll also remember the name the next time they call to book an escort.

Now that we have established who will be answering the phones, it's time to discuss how to answer the phones.

How do I answer the phone? What do I say?

When you answer, your greeting should alert the caller that he/she has reached a business and not someone's personal number. If you just say "hello" the caller may hang-up, believing it possible that they have reached a wrong number.

I have always answered: "Hello, can I help you?"

Other possible greetings include:

"Service." – and then let the caller speak, but if they do not speak, then add "Can I help you?"

"Service, can I help you?"

"Good evening, can I help you?" (depending on time of day)

Hopefully you listened to what other bookers said when answering when you researched prices. There are many ways to answer the phone, as long as you do not just say "hello" it will sound like a business to the caller. If the caller asks: "Is this Ardvark?" Your response should be: "Yes, this is the service, can I help you?" The reason for this is that you sure don't want to tell the caller that they have reached a wrong number, and it's apparent that their eyes just didn't focus on the number near the name, but never actually state that it is Ardvark.

I have known of escort business owners that never answered the phones, and I have done this on occasion as well. The lines are all put on voicemail and the message is retrieved immediately. This is intended for deception – if your lines are never actually answered, no one can know if you're really in business or not, or if you ever respond to a message. An owner could do this for several reasons, and usually it's done to screen calls and selectively return calls.

I know of an escort service owner that used to have the phones forever on voicemail for other reasons entirely though. Cindy would listen to the voice mail, and if the potential client was in a hotel, she just sent an escort, never calling him back. She had several escorts that hung-out in Orlando's International Drive/Lake Buena Vista resort area. I discovered this when her escorts pretended to be from my service and took the clients. Example:

The potential client is calling around for rates and availability. I answer, state a rate, and then book the client. I ask him what type or age range he is seeking, he states his preferences, and I describe Tanya. I state that I will have Tanya call him within 5 minutes and it will take her about 45 minutes to get to his room. What I do not know is that he called other agencies to inquire before he booked with me, and otherwise this would be immaterial anyway. About 20 minutes later he hears a knock on the door, but thinks that Tanya is early, so he questions, "Tanya?" The girl from the other agency responds that "yes, it's Tanya" and he opens the door. He asks, "Are you from Valentine's?" thinking that she doesn't look like the escort I described or sound like the escort he spoke with, but she smoothes it over some way; any way for that matter, and says anything necessary to collect the money. Ten minutes later there's a knock on the door, and it's Tanya. He looks through the peephole and realizes that this is the Tanya that he spoke with and was expecting. At this point he is confused. Before you know it, the other girl is blaming him for calling multiple services and booking appointments, and she's moving quickly out the door.

Of course this other girl has taken the money with her, so now the guy has no way to pay Tanya. Tanya leaves. We all lose, except Cindy's rip-off operation. They did this for years, and cost me too many calls. I fixed them a few times though. The client can't be blamed as all he did was leave a message on Cindy's line, and no one ever returned his call.

So, you can keep your phones on voicemail and selectively return calls if you want to, but please don't be another Cindy and just send the escorts uninvited. Perhaps you will choose to do this with your lines once in a while to remain somewhat elusive. I would advise voicemail until the yellow pages are distributed and you're fully in business.

If you do leave your phones on voicemail, you will want to use the following message or some variation thereof. Make sure that the message is recorded by someone with a sexy female voice:

"Hi. You have reached the service. Please leave your name, telephone number, and if you leave a hotel number, include the name the room is registered to and the room number. We will return your call within 5 minutes. Thank you."

Say this somewhat fast – don't be speedy gonzalez or anything, just practice and state it clearly and quickly. No one listens to long, drawn-out greetings. Realize that if the potential client leaves his name as "Joe, room 1221 at the Dolphin, 407-934-4000," you will never reach him. Most good hotels will not connect you to a room unless you have the name of the registered guest, so state **"the name the room is registered to"** clearly.

In short time you will have your dialogue exactly how you want it. In the meantime, here are some answers beyond the initial greeting and voicemail setup:

Caller #1 (a more complicated call):

Me: "Hello, can I help you?"

Caller: "What are your rates?"

Me: "The rate is $400 **cash** for an hour." (emphasize "cash")

Caller: "Who do you have available?" (never start rolling off descriptions)

Me: "The escorts are ages 24 to 45, American, Latina, Caribbean, and Russian. We have all types of ladies available. Where are you located?" (ask him a question at the end of your statement)

Caller: "I am staying at the *Hilton* downtown." (now I know that I want to book him − if he was staying at the *Motel 6*, I probably would not)

Me: "Is this for now, or did you want to make an appointment for later?" (you can't describe an escort until you know when it's for)

Caller: "I have a 9pm dinner reservation downstairs at the *Bistro*, so I'd like someone to join me. I hate dining alone, but I do need to get up early so it won't be a late night."

Me: "What type of lady do you prefer? Any particular age group or other important attributes?" (always get the client to state the type he is looking for)

Caller: "Well, I do want someone in her thirties and well-built, but other than this, I am open to your suggestion."

Me: "I would recommend Nina. She is 36 years, 5'9", 128, and has shoulder length natural blonde hair. She is a 36D-26-36 and is often requested. Most people that meet Nina want to see her again."

Caller: "Okay, Nina sounds fine."

Me: "I can give you a rate of $1000, cash only as we do not accept credit cards, for 3 hours." (I did this anticipating that he wanted Nina to return to the room with him after dinner – offering more hours usually works when the client wants company for dinner)

Caller: "That's fine. Can you have Nina call me?" (He is not into discussing money and that's a good thing)

Me: "Certainly. Let me get some information first, and then I will have Nina call you. What is your name?"

Caller: "Joe"

Me: "And your last name Joe?"

Caller: "Schnitell – s-c-h-n-i-t-e-l-l. I am in room 1432."

Me: "Do you have the telephone number at the *Hilton* Joe?" (I ask even though I know every number for every hotel in Miami by memory – I really used to)

Joe: "Sure. It is 555-555-5555, but I would prefer that Nina called my cellular. The number is 999-999-9999."

Me: "Okay. I'll call you right back in the room – I must verify that you are there, and then I will have Nina reach you on your cell-phone." (always verify that Joe is actually in the hotel and the room is registered in his name). "My name is Laura, and I will call you within a couple of minutes Joe."

Joe: "Thank you."

Now I call Joe back in his room, and that is when I ask a few additional questions so I'm satisfied that Joe has good intentions. I do not ask much until I know who I'm talking to though. An alternate way of booking Joe is to not describe any escort until you call him back in his room. If I have any idea that the caller is fooling around or is not really where they say they are, I will not describe escorts without calling him back. If I think Joe is okay, or I see the downtown *Hilton* telephone number on the caller ID, I'll just go ahead and have a conversation. This "caller #1" dialogue continues in **Verifying Clients**.

Caller #2

Me: "Good evening. Can I help you?"

Caller: "Who do you have available tonight?" (not a proper question at this point)

Me: "We have all types of escorts available sir – American, Latina, Caribbean, and Russian, ages 24 to 45 at this time. Have you used this service before?" (I ask this because he tried to come-off like he knows us)

Caller: "No I haven't. I want a hot blonde." (I know I didn't ask and I'm not describing anyone to this guy until I call him back)

Me: "Is this for now or some other time? Where are you located?"

Caller: "I'm in Cutler Ridge and yes it's for now." (he doesn't even know the rate and Cutler Ridge covers a large geographical area in South Miami-Dade County)

Me: "The rate is $400, cash only, for one hour. I can call you back and let you know who specifically is available." (he never even asked the rate)

Caller: "Never mind. That's too much."

Me: "Have a great night."

This caller was most likely fooling around to begin with. Look at what he stated – hopefully you understand why I say this. You will get calls like this. Sometimes the caller just wants you to run off a list of girls and descriptions. Do not oblige this type of caller. Use caution and offer as little information as possible.

Caller #3

Me: "Service, can I help you?"

Caller: "I'd like to make an appointment. How long does it take to get someone here?" (sounds like he just wants the fastest possible escort)

Me: "Depending where you are, I would say that it will take about an hour to get just about any escort to any part of the area. Where are you?" (I can see on the caller ID that he is at a *Marriott* downtown)

Caller: "I'm at the Miami *Marriott*. Can't you get anyone here in less time than that?" (I won't bother establishing exactly which *Marriott* for a few reasons)

Me: "It usually takes around an hour. There is traffic in Miami sir, and these are women; they take a few minutes to get out the door. This isn't a pizza delivery." (I say this in a joking way, but it's true)

Caller: "I do understand, it's just that I have an appointment and I'm jammed on time. Does it always take that long?"

Me: "Yes, or close to it. Our rate is $400 cash for an hour, I'm Laura, and I will be answering until 5am. Please give me a call when you have time to relax for a bit." (I state this nicely and in a relaxing, slow, and joking voice. I want him to call back later, and he probably will. They usually do)

Caller: "Thank you Laura. If I can manage it I will call you when I'm finished with my meeting and dinner." (he is obviously here on business)

Me: "Have a nice evening. I'll look forward to hearing from you later." (I leave him with this thought on his mind)

Always be nice to the callers, unless of course you think that they're fooling around and wasting your time – if that is the case, just get them off the phone as you don't need them to tie up the line – Often callers that sound like our Caller #3 will call back, so you haven't wasted your time with this. In smaller metropolitan areas or small cities, a service can often get an escort there in 30 minutes, and Caller #3 probably has no idea how spread out the area is and the added time involved in parking and getting to the room. This "caller #3 dialogue continues in **Verifying Clients**.

Caller #4

Me: "Good evening. Can I help you?"

Caller: "What are your rates?"

Me: "The rate is $400 cash for one hour or $700 for 2 hours." (sometimes it's a good idea to throw in the 2 hour rate)

Caller: "I'd like to make an appointment. How long will it take to get someone here?" (I have no idea where "here" is as he's calling from an out-of-town cell-phone)

Me: "It usually takes about an hour to get just about any escort to any part of the area. Where are you located?"

Caller: "I'm at the *Raleigh* in South Beach." (if it's midnight on a Saturday night, traffic in South Beach is atrocious – never forget about traffic – and it's not simple to park and get in the hotel either)

Me: "It could take up to an hour and a half due to traffic, parking, and getting to your room. Is this okay?" (if it's not okay I really can't help him because I don't promise times that I cannot meet)

Caller: (laughs) "Yes, you're right. Sure, as long as you are pretty sure that she can make it in 90 minutes. I'm not really in a hurry." (we would hope he's not in a hurry as we would like to book him for the two hours)

Me: "I don't think the 90 minutes will be a problem for anyone. What type of escort are you looking for? Any particular age group?"

Caller: "I'd really like someone in their mid-twenties, Latina, on the slender side, if you have someone like this available."

Me: "I will recommend Carmen. She is 24 in age, 5'7", 115, slender and beautiful. Carmen has long natural dark hair. (it's a good idea to describe the person that you want to send at this point)

Caller: "Sounds wonderful. Can you have her call me?"

Me: "Certainly Carmen will call you. I need to get some information, call your room to verify that you are there, and then Carmen will call you and let you know exactly how long it will take for her to get to you. What is your name?"

Caller: "Thor Svernsen"

Me: "Please spell your last name Thor."

Thor: "S-v-e-r-n-s-e-n. I am in room 242."

Me: "Is the room registered to your name Thor?" (I need to know because if it isn't, I'll never get through)

Thor: "Yes. It is in my name."

Me: "My name is Laura and I will call you right back Thor. I do just need to make sure that you are in the room." (I didn't ask the hotel phone number because I can get it quickly if I don't know it, and Thor is obviously from another country and I don't want to put him through the trouble of finding it)

Thor: "I will expect your call."

Now I will call Thor back in his room. I do need to ask a couple of questions and I'll try to book him for the 2 hours. He's from another country (I think at this point) and he probably wants an escort for more than 1 hour. This dialogue with "caller #4" continues in **Verifying Clients**.

Caller #5

Me: "Good evening. Can I help you?"

Caller: "We want an escort to come out. What are your rates?"

Me: "How many people are there?" (he did say "we")

Caller: "I'm alone."

Me: "It's $700 cash for an hour." (he is not alone so I want to discourage him instead of being rude about it)

Caller: "What? That's crazy."

Me: "Sorry that I can't help you. Have a nice evening."

I chose to be polite because I'm busy and do not have time to deal with idiots in groups that claim they are alone. I always listen for sounds of another person being present when I'm on the phone with a caller, but in this case he said "we" and I doubt that he has a mouse in his pocket. I also do not want them getting angry and calling 20 more times.

Caller #6

Me: "Good evening. Can I help you?"

Caller: "What are your rates?"

Me: "The rate is $400 cash only for one hour."

Caller: "Is this full service?" (that is a term that is frequently used when a caller wants to be sure sex is included)

Me: "Sir, this is escorts by the hour. You are paying for the escort's time and company."

Caller: "Are you saying that full service costs more?" (I'm not saying anything except what I said)

Me: Click

I hung-up on this caller because I already told him once what service the agency offered. There is no reason to get involved in a word game. There is also no reason for me to repeat myself. If he called back and asked why I hung-up on him, I'd simply say: "I'm sorry that we can't help you. Have a nice night." I would then hang-up again. Never compromise yourself, the escort, or the business to book one idiot, and never explain yourself.

Caller #7

Me: "Service, can I help you?"

Caller: "I would like an escort to come over. What do you charge?"

Me: "The rate is $400 cash for one hour and it will take around an hour for any escort to get there."

Caller: "That's fine. Who do you have available?"

Me: "The escorts are ages 21 to 45, American, Latina, and Caribbean at this time. Are you in a hotel or a residence?" (I see that he is calling from a Miami number and I do not recognize it as a hotel number)

Caller: "I'm in my house, in the Grove." (He's referring to Coconut Grove. Most residences in the Grove are at least better than average, and he stated "house" – this is something that I can verify without asking anymore questions)

Me: "What type and age of an escort are you looking for?"

Caller: "Someone in their late thirties or early forties that's not in a hurry."

Me: "I definitely recommend Monica. She is 41 years, 5'8", 125, and she has shoulder length natural brown hair. Most people that see Monica request to see her again."

Caller: "She sounds nice. What do you need?"

Me: "Your name?"

Caller: "Jack Smith"

Me: "Is Smith actually your last name?" (I'm asking because it's common)

Caller: "Believe it or not, that's my name."

Me: "Okay Jack. What is your address?"

Jack: "I'm at 455 Bayridge Road."

Me: "That is a house, correct?" (I want to be sure)

Jack: "Yes it is."

Me: "Would you like Monica to call the number that you called from?"

Jack: "Please."

Me: "My name is Laura, Jack, and I will have Monica call you within 5 minutes."

Clients in houses are usually simple to verify, Jack was nice, and he didn't ask anything off the wall. He sounds older – perhaps 60s. Just for good measure, I will verify one fact before I call Monica. This dialogue with "caller #7" continues in **Verifying Clients**.

Caller #8

Me: "Good evening, can I help you?"

Caller: "We need a girl to come over and dance at a bachelor party, maybe two girls."

Me: "When is this for sir?" (I hear the party going on in the background)

Caller: "As soon as possible. We're all here now." (of course I knew that)

Me: "I am sorry, but we do require at least 24 hours notice for a party booking, otherwise this is only one escort seeing one gentleman. It's private only."

Caller: "Where can I call to get someone now?" (I've never been anyone's free referral service and it's never intelligent to acknowledge knowing people at another agency)

Me: "I have no idea. I know nothing about any other agency."

It is a good idea to book parties; however, dancers that do parties require notice for preparation and will rarely go to a last minute appointment. It is a good idea to have at least two dancers that you can call for an advance party booking, but they will quickly dump you if you don't book it correctly, which translates to how they want it booked, and give them at least 1 day notice. Potential clients know well in advance if they're having a bachelor party, so there's no valid excuse for the "now" mentality. I will discuss booking parties towards the end of this chapter.

Caller #9

Me: "Good evening, can I help you?"

Caller: "I want someone to come to my apartment. What do you charge?" (I am always cautious when booking anyone in an apartment and I'm listening closely for background noises)

Me: "The rate is $400 cash only for one hour, and it will take 45 minutes to an hour to get anyone there."

Caller: "Okay. I want a young blonde. Who do you have?"

Me: "I can give you a call back and let you know who specifically is available. What is your number?" (I see it on the caller ID, but I want him to repeat it so I know that he knows it)

Caller: "It's 305-555-3333."

Me: "I will give you a call right back and let you know who is available." (if I heard background issues, I'll never call him back, but if not, I'll give it a try)

Booking clients in apartments requires some skill – don't get me wrong, you can book anyone; however, you should know something about the caller and that's not easy with an apartment. When you know something about a caller he will think twice about causing any problem for the escort, or even harming her. I will question this guy more when I call him back. This "caller #9" dialogue continues in **Verifying Clients**.

The caller dialogues cover the situations that you will encounter most often. Of course there other situations that are infrequent, and some so odd that no one could dream it up to address it. Every person that calls the agency is an individual. You must understand that and treat each caller individually. Really listen to each person that calls you. Most important, always remember that it's up to you if an escort goes to see a caller or not. Never let anyone bully you into sending an escort if you don't want to. You are driving the stagecoach here. You are in control of the situation. Sometimes you won't need to ask a caller much and other times you'll feel the need to question for 20 minutes. The idea is to question until you feel secure in booking the caller and you believe that the situation is what it is, and the caller doesn't have ulterior motives.

I must tell you that when I learned to answer escort lines in Miami back in the 1980s, we did nothing more than call 411 and confirm that the phone number was listed at the address the caller gave us. We did at least do this though, and many services didn't bother with even this simple check. We quickly developed repeats (clients that called two or more times and we knew that they were okay) and pursued more hours. It was not unheard of to have an escort at a call for three days, but then this was Miami in the 80s, the era of the cocaine cowboys. Services also had "blacklists" and usually shared information with the other services.

Today is different in that information is rarely traded between services and few agencies have contact with other agencies. The entire structure of the business has changed. I was taught to book in volume and to get the client's information and get him off of the phone quickly. If it took five minutes to book a call it was three minutes too long. We booked just about everyone that called. Money, and lots of it, could be found in the seediest of places. A dumpy apartment could be the next five hour call. I doubt that this has changed much, but what has changed is that agencies are weary of potential problems. This is for the better.

My cautious method of questioning until I'm satisfied that the caller has no ulterior motives is just my method. Obviously you can develop your own method in short time. Answering escort lines is not rocket science, and less questioning usually equals more calls booked. The only real requirement here is that you are as sure as possible that the caller is really where they're saying they are at. That does mean you should call a client in a hotel back in his room before calling the escort. It also means that verifying property ownership is a good idea, but you could also just dial 411 and confirm that an address connects to a phone number, if the caller has a landline in the apartment or house. If you do none of the above, the escorts will quickly tire and jump ship as you'll have too many bad calls. When I use the phrase "bad calls" it usually means calls where the caller is not there and no one answers the door. It can also mean dangerous calls.

Now I will move on to a discussion of the information to ask a potential clients and ways to verify that info.

Verifying Clients: Information to ask

It takes years of experience to know if a caller is good by voice alone and without bothering to check him out, so I will give you a list of ways that you can verify information on a potential client. None of these methods are foolproof, so do not treat any as if it were. Listening to the caller is the most important tool in your toolbox.

Do not consider using any service or program that claims to verify clients for you. Never give a client's, or a potential client's, information to any third party. Doing so is no different than creating a client list and faxing a copy to the local police or even the feds.

The goals of verifying a client are that the client is really just seeking an escort for an hour and has no ulterior motives and to be sure the client is not a cop working an undercover operation. Don't get me wrong on the cop thing – I have helped cops before because cops are people too, but you do not want to help one set the escort up – these are two different topics. It is not necessarily that the escort will do anything illegal, and it's more that agents with an undercover operation would find something to charge her with whether she did or not.

Residences and hotels are like two different species when it comes to verifying callers, so I will discuss them separately.

Residences

The best way to check a caller that's in a house or a condominium is to go to the property appraiser website for the county area, in this case the Miami-Dade County Property Appraiser. The website can be found at:

http://www.miamidade.gov/pa/property_search.asp

You can search by name or by address. Most areas around the country have the property information online, so this type of search also can work on a caller in a hotel. I have searched remote areas in New York to see if there was any property in a potential client's name, but mostly I did this only because I was not clear on the person, and perhaps didn't believe the information that I was given.

Another way to search is simply to *Google* the caller's first and last name. You would be surprised how much information is available. Your caller could be a scientist that just gave a speech at a nearby university. When a caller is in a house or a condo, this is used in conjunction with a property search if you don't find the answers you seek by searching property. Note that you never want to tell the potential client that you searched for their private information anywhere, as it's likely that they would pass on your agency. These type of searches take all of three minutes so there's no delay in sending an escort if the caller sounds okay otherwise.

If the caller is in an apartment, the property search stuff is null and void as renters are not listed. It is really hard to be sure about a caller in an apartment, and often I just passed on apartments, unless of course I knew the client. These days most potential clients call you from a wireless phone, and many do not have a landline installed, so in an apartment situation you can't be sure that the person is even there. It could be an idiot fooling around or another agency that wants to see you fail by sending your escorts on wild goose chases. The bottom line is that you really need to be sure that a client is where they say they are before sending an escort.

Sometimes it works to ask the caller: "What type of business are you in?" If the caller says that he works for himself or owns his own business of whatever type, checking is easy. Go to the Florida Department of State, Division of Corporations website (most states have them). You can search documents by name, but make sure that you check "Corporations etc..." and "Fictitious Names etc..." before you consider the caller a liar. No telling how his business is set-up. The website can be found at:

http://www.sunbiz.org

Also, if the caller claims to be a professional of any type, such as a physician, an attorney, a realtor, an auctioneer etc... you can easily check the Florida

Department of Business and Professional Regulation (DBPR) website. If the caller's claimed business is regulated by the state, they will have a license that is findable in this database. For an attorney you would want to check the Florida Bar Association website and click the "find a lawyer" link. Once again, most states have the same type of websites, though sometimes the name of the government agency can be different. The websites:

http://www.myfloridalicense.com/wl11.asp (DBPR)
http://www.floridabar.org (Florida Bar)

All of this can be applied to clients in hotels also as it's usually as easy to check the state government websites in the state that the caller is from.

It is important to keep questioning until you are satisfied, and realize that you will not help everyone that calls. The idea is to book all the calls that you can, but to avoid problems at all costs. I did have an escort that ended-up in a problem in a house, a very nice house at that, but the problem was not foreseeable and we both knew enough about the guy to do something about it if she wanted to. When I state that the problem wasn't foreseeable it's because the guy owned a restaurant, had called once before and saw the same escort for two hours – she stated that they played pool for most of the time and he was a gentleman and nice to her. The next time he called he requested her and was anything but a gentleman. She was the only escort he ever saw through my agency, so there was no one to compare notes with concerning his demeanor and actions.

Hotels

I always found booking a client in a hotel to be easier. To begin with, when you ask the caller his name, also ask if the room is registered to his name. If necessary, explain to the caller that neither you nor the escort will ever reach him in his room if you do not have the correct name. Assure him that you do not save his information in any list or book, and don't save it once the call is over. If you don't have the name the room is registered to, you will usually not get through, especially at 2am. If it is daytime or in the evening and you're responding to a voicemail wherein the caller didn't leave a last name, try it by asking for the room number, and muttering a created name if the operator asks for the name of the guest. Sometimes hotel operators are too busy to bother checking, but sometimes they check.

If the caller claims to be someone other than the name the room is registered to, it's usually best to let it go. He is as cautious as you are. So if the room is registered to Jim Horst and the client claims to be Robert Bell, he's just covering his ass. When you give the call to the escort explain the discrepancy – experienced escorts are used to this. When she sees his ID states Jim Horst, she will know why. Be upfront and honest with the escorts.

When you are booking the caller in a hotel you will also ask him where he is from. If he's not easily verifiable, as an attorney or doctor is, then try searching *Google* for the name and state or country. Search through the pages that show in the search results and you will likely find some mention of this caller that allows you to have some level of certainty that the caller and the person referred to are one and the same.

When you ask the caller where he is from it also has other purpose – you follow with the question: "So you can show the escort a driver's license from Maine (or wherever)?" Most clients of escort services expect you to ask this and expect to show an escort ID, be it a passport or a driver's license. If the caller states that he has no ID, you know he is full of crap because he couldn't check-in the hotel or fly without ID.

Asking the caller what line of business he is in is not intrusive – you are not asking for his work information or where specifically he works. Do not let anyone tell you that the information is intrusive. Think about that for a minute. Always keep asking questions until you are satisfied. I never, in 10 years of business, had any problem with an escort being harmed in a hotel. I booked mostly hotels.

Verifying Clients: The Dialogues Revisited

Caller #1

Me: "This is Laura. I just have to make sure you're really there Joe. I meant to ask you before, but what line of business are you in?" (I sort of toss it in after I call Joe back)

Joe: "I'm really here." (laughing) "Does that matter?"

Me: "No. I'm only asking so that I know you intend no harm – legal or otherwise –I always spend a few minutes getting to know a person. I also ask that you show Nina a driver's license."

Joe: "I'm in the medical field and yes, the license is not an issue." (he sounds like he is so I won't take it any further, and he sounds more paranoid than I am which is always good)

Me: "Thank you Joe. You do understand that this is cash only and we do not take credit cards?" (since I quoted Joe $1000 for 3 hours I won't restate that figure but I reiterate **cash**)

Joe: "Wouldn't have it any other way." (smart man)

Me: "I will have Nina call you right away. Have a great night." (I call Nina right away)

I inform the escort that I booked this call for $1000 cash for 3 hours, and supposedly Joe has a dinner reservation at a restaurant in the hotel. She will collect the quoted amount shortly after arrival, check Joe's license, and call me to check-in – that is when the time starts. She will call from the hotel room phone, or if that is not an option, she'll call from Joe's cellular phone, but she will not call from her phone in case she must hand the phone to Joe and walk out the door in the same moment.

When the escort calls to check-in, I will ask her, "Is everything okay?" Now this is a loaded question and it means: 1) Did she check the driver's license and the name is the same name that the room is registered to? 2) Did Joe pay her the $1000 cash as expected? and 3) Everything looks okay and he seems nice enough. In this case I will confirm that she collected what she was supposed to collect because the figure is for several hours.

If anything doesn't seem right she knows to speak-up at this point. She will alert me by sounding different when I ask if everything is okay. She might even say: "I think so" or make an odd sound, like "umhum" or say "sure." If she sounds weird, I would ask her if they're going to the restaurant. If she responded no, that Joe changed his mind, I would ask her to put him on the phone. After I talk to Joe again, regardless of the outcome, I would ask him to put Nina on the phone. If I was not 100% satisfied with his answer, I would instruct Nina to keep 20 to $50 for herself, hand the rest back to Joe, and exit after handing him the phone and while I'm speaking with him. All of this is unlikely though: it is a rare occurrence with someone like Joe.

Caller #3

Our "caller #3" was the man in a hurry at the *Marriott* downtown. He calls back much later, say 1AM, which is 5 hours later. I liked him and now the story fits – he had plenty of time to finish a meeting and dinner, and now he seeks an escort. If he called back two hours after the original call, I would doubt the timing enough to question him in-depth. Business engagements just do not go that quickly.

Me: "Hello, can I help you?"

Caller: "Hi Laura. We spoke earlier in the evening, and I'm all done with business and ready to relax. Who do you have available?"

Me: "Please refresh my memory dear – where are you?" (I already knew exactly who he was when I saw the hotel on the caller ID, and positively knew when he called me Laura as I told him my name earlier)

Caller: "I'm at the Miami *Marriott*, Laura. When I called before I was in a hurry."

Me: "Of course I remember. It will probably take an hour to get just about any escort there. What type of escort are you looking for?"

Caller: "I'd really like to see a Latina lady if that's possible, probably younger rather than older."

Me: "I do have Carmen available. She is 24, 5'7", 115, and she has long dark hair. If you would like, I can have Carmen give you a call?" (I know that Carmen is not far away and she fits the request, so she is the one I try to send)

Caller: "Carmen sounds great. Please have her call me."

Me: "Just a few questions first. What is your name?"

Caller: "Jake Schmidt. I'm in room 222."

Me: "Okay Jake, where are you from?"

Jake: "I live in Houston. I can show her a license. I know how it works." (good – he saved me one question anyway)

Me: "And are you at the hotel on business Jake? What type of business are you in?" (he already said he was here on business, so if he now claims to be a tourist I have a list of questions, but probably wouldn't book him)

Jake: "I'm an attorney Laura. Is that okay?"

Me: (laughing) "Of course it's okay. We love attorneys here! I will have Carmen call you right away Jake, and it shouldn't take her much over 30 minutes to get there." (I try to joke with clients if it's the right time. Because he's an attorney, I won't bother to ask anything else. Before I call Carmen I'll *Google* "Jake Schmidt attorney Texas" and make sure that I find something with his name and office information, or an article about him; just something)

This caller is a "no problem" type of client. He has more to lose than we do. If he likes Carmen, and he will as I chose her mainly because I often get repeat requests for her, he will probably call me again tomorrow for Carmen or someone else. When I call Carmen I will inform her of the earlier call, that he is an attorney from Texas, and I'll ask her to reiterate the **cash** part. Nothing pisses me off more than some idiot claiming he thought we took credit cards, so that's why I say it more than once or have the escort follow-up and state it the second time.

Caller #4

Me: "Hello. I need the room registered to Thor Svernsen please."

Hotel operator: "Please spell the last name."

Me: "S-v-e-r-n-s-e-n."

Hotel operator: "I'll put you through to Mr. Svern-sen's room. One moment please."

Me: "This is Laura with the service Thor. I just wanted to make sure that you are there. Where are you from Thor?"

Thor: "Hello Laura. I am from Sweden."

Me: "Will you be able to show Carmen a passport Thor?"

Thor: "Of course Laura. Please just send her over."

Me: "I will have her call you and let you know how long she will be Thor. Are you here for business or pleasure?" (I throw that in after responding to his question)

Thor: "I am vacationing in Miami. I will be here for 10 more days. (If he said that he was here on business I would doubt him as the *Raleigh* in South Beach is not a business hotel for the most part)

Me: "I do hope that you have a great time in Miami Thor. It is the best place to vacation! I'll have Carmen call right away."

Thor is one of the many international tourists that vacation in Miami, and come with plenty of money. If I'm lucky he will call me again each day that he's in town. This is really an easy book. The hotel is top shelf and money flows in South Beach. I will have Carmen reiterate the **cash** part when she calls back. If he really likes her, he will probably have her stay for a second hour, and if he asks for a break in the rate, I'll have Carmen tell him that since it's the second hour, we can charge $300. This will make him happy, but we do stress that the deal is only on the second hour. If he asked for the $300 rate when he called the following evening, I would offer a rate of $700 for two hours or $350 for one hour, but not $300 for only one hour.

Caller #7

I do not bother to call Jack Smith back as I quickly verified that he is the owner of the property at 455 Bayridge Road in the Grove. I also know, from the Property Appraiser's website, that it is a million$ property. I just call Monica and tell her to call Jack right away. If the address didn't verify, I'd have to call Jack back and get a correct name, or toss the call. I would never tell Jack how I know that Smith is not his name though. I already know what name I want to hear when I call back – the name of the listed property owner.

Caller #9

Me: "Hello, this is Laura with the service. I need to ask a few questions before I can send an escort. What is your name?" (I'm ignoring his description request for the moment)

Caller: "Manny Bartoman. Do you have a young blonde available?"

Me: "Of course we do Manny. I have Julie. She is 21 years, 5'6", 120, and she has long natural blonde hair. Is this for now?" (I got the description out of the way in case I do want to book him. Why have him ask again and again?)

Manny: "Julie sounds good, but who else do you have?" (no more descriptions for the moment)

Me: "Well Manny, first give me your address so that I know where you are." (more so I know if I'd send anyone to the area or not)

Manny: "I'm at 1438 N.W. 6th Avenue near down-town. I'm in apartment 211." (this area can be semi-dangerous)

Me: "I am sorry Manny, but I really can't send any-one to that area. The only way I can help you is if you check into a hotel, and it needs to be a *Holiday Inn* or better – no *Days Inns*." (Days Inns are okay in some areas, but not really in Miami)

Manny: "That's not right. There's nothing wrong with my apartment."

Me: "I am sure there's not, but there's too much crime in the area for us. I know where you are dear – I've lived here most of my life. If you decide to check into a hotel, please do call me back." (even if I'd lived in Miami for 2 months I'd know better than to send a girl to that area, especially to an apartment. A house, maybe, it would depend entirely on the person. An apartment first depends on the area, then on the person)

There are some really great people that call from apartments, but we must be careful, so with an apartment, it must be in a safe neighborhood. If it is we then move on to analyzing the person: What line of business is he in? Is it verifiable? If I can't verify anything on an apartment caller, I usually do not send an escort. Of course there are always exceptions.

Discovering and Preventing Theft

Most people that you encounter in the escort business would like to steal your money, so it's up to you to discover what they are up to and stop them. Most information in relation to theft is in the chapter, *The Escorts*, as the escorts are the main thieves that you will contend with. Bookers and phone people also steal though; some worse than others. The best advice that I can give you is to run the phones yourself and maintain complete control over your own operation. If there are two people embarking on this business venture it is unlikely that you will ever have a need for an outsider to book your calls. If you're alone in this, realize that you can answer the phone doing almost anything and pay more attention only when you are actually booking the call. If you are alone you will want to consider the best hours to operate and answer yourself during those hours, say 6pm until 4am. Just leave it on voicemail the rest of the time and return calls when you start answering for the night.

There are too many problems involved in having an outsider (not a close friend or a relative) answer your lines. One problem is that these people do make commissions, although usually they also receive daily pay, but the commission accounts for much more and they are motivated to book. That might sound great from a sales perspective, but the reality is that you have no real clue what the booker is saying in order to book your calls. He or she could say anything as it's unlikely for the booker to feel the legal repercussions. It is your ass on the line, so be careful who you hand it to: the phone account is in your name, or your corporation's name. In the end it is you that will pay.

I was a booking agent in Miami long before I opened services in Orlando. The owner of the agency did something terrible to me – she had no scruples, and quite frankly, she was a bitch. Well, I fixed her. The last two months that I worked for her I was working with a friend/escort that also despised her, and we split Kim's fees between us while I told Kim that there were no calls whenever she questioned me. It was my friend's idea whereas I wanted to tell Kim to drop dead. My friend convinced me that we would all be broke if I did that and it was best to just pay her back for her dirty deeds. I won't reveal what she did to me as it's too embarrassing for a book, but it was unexpected, stupid, and dirty. Kim should have known better than to screw over the one honest person in her life, and the one that answered her phones 24/7 while she was partying out-of-state.

The moral of that story is that if you are going to pay a booker that you meet in the course of this business, do not screw the booker over. Payback is a bitch.

When I went into business in Orlando, I hired the wife of an acquaintance to book calls on the late shift, from 9-10pm until 5-6am. I paid Lisa well – when all was said and done, she made more than I did (I had all the expenses) – and she had zero experience. I taught her everything and soon she considered herself indispensable; this was her mistake. One day Lisa, prompted by her husband, decided to demand more money from me, and rather than play the extortion game I opted to say goodbye. She followed our parting by trashing me to anyone that would listen: other escort service owners; the escorts that worked with **my business**; and even the police. Suffice it to say that I still had friends and Lisa soon moved back to Ohio. I took care of her legally, but it was far from easy. Don't invite a Lisa into your life. Just answer your own phones.

Imagine how simple it is for a booker to hire one extra escort without your knowledge – the escort is usually his/her friend – and give her several calls a day, keeping the fees. It is so easy that the booker could also run a shadow service off of your agency. Why have only one shadow escort when you can have three? Since you are not entering the escort business to donate your money to thieves, simply pass on outsider booking agents.

On Booking Parties

It is a good idea to have a couple of dancers from the clubs that you can call for parties. The dancers always know exactly what they're doing and advise you as to how much notice is necessary, what they want you to say to the client as far as pay and tips are concerned, and the number of people that is acceptable or if they must work with 1 or 2 other dancers. Every detail of the party will be handled by the dancers except the actual booking and rate quote. Of course you must verify the information before notifying the dancer of the booking. You will also call the contact person to confirm the day before. Most often the dancers have a man that will go with them to parties, but if not, you must find someone or go yourself.

This is not an area of the business that you want to ignore. You can book several parties a week. You can also offer a stripper with a message type of service, like the strip-o-grams in the past. It is a safe, legal money maker. Your involvement will usually be minimal as the dancers prefer to control the entire gig. In this case, you let them and just collect your fee later. Finding dancers to work with is easy: just go to the men's clubs and when you see a likely candidate, give her a business card wrapped in the bill/tip. You might also note on the back of the card that you need a couple of dancers to call for parties only (if she wanted to escort she would be already). If the particular dancer is not interested, she will probably pass your card on to a dancer that is. Do not let management in the club view you doing this or they will throw you out.

On Drivers

You do not need or want anyone to work for the agency as a driver. You may have escorts that have their own driver, and that is fine, but the agency only has escorts that are independent, so we are not going to drive them around. There are agencies that hire a driver and make the escorts ride with the driver all night, but I consider this ridiculous. No woman with brains is going to ride around with a bunch of strangers all night, and we only have intelligent escorts. Often these agency drivers sell drugs and make moves on the escorts. In general, this is a lousy way to run a service.

If there are two of you running this show, one of you will be meeting the escorts after calls and picking up fees, interviewing escorts, catching the thieves, and generally doing the late running around. The other would do best to stay behind the scene, answer phones, deal with the ads, taxes etc.... If you are alone in this venture, once you are busy, you'll need a trusted driver/collector to collect fees and do the running, but never to drive the escorts anywhere.

A few important notes:

You will instruct every escort to call you when she is available and to call and let you know when she needs to be off for any reason. What you do not want is to describe an escort to a client, call her, and she gives you some explanation of why she can't go for 3 hours. This will screw you up! Do not let them do it. The policy is call on and to call off. If you describe an escort to a client and this happens, it means that you must call the client back again and describe a different escort, and you always chance losing the call when you do that. This is supposed to go smoothly: You describe the escort to the client and he agrees; You dial the escort that is supposed to be available; The escort answers, takes the information, and calls the client back; The escort calls you and tells you that she is on her way; The escort calls to check-in at the client's location. Any variation, such as the escort calling you and telling you that he doesn't want her to come over until three hours later, is a problem. When you booked the client, he stated that it was for now, and not three hours later. Either she is stealing the call or she has something else to do for the next three hours, and neither is acceptable. With any escort that you do not know well enough to trust, do not have her call unless it's you hook the call up with 3-way calling. With a hotel you must give the escort the information, but if you consider it possible that she will steal the call (if she's new and you don't know her), the call can be on a three-way and you can always drive to the hotel if she doesn't call to check-in with you.

When you do have an escort call the client back (you won't all the time), make sure that you instruct her to state: "Did the agency tell you that it is cash only and I cannot accept credit cards?" The reason for this is so that she doesn't arrive and encounter a client claiming the service never said it was cash only. You know that you said it, and probably tossed it in the conversation more than once. The escort should also know that you have already said it. Doing it this way prevents later problems.

Always seriously consider what the escort says about the client after she calls him back. If you know the escort well enough to know that she would never try to steal your fee, you should believe what she says. If you aren't sure, you can follow-up and find out if she's stealing the client. But then again, if you do not know her well enough to believe her, she should not have been given the phone number any-way. This is the situation wherein the escort doesn't call the client. You can have someone call and pretend to be her – I used to do that often with new escorts. If it's a hotel call it is easy to see if she went there when she told you the client cancelled. If you are really unsure of her, you can instruct her to call you from the hotel lobby for the room number. This topic is addressed more in *The Escorts*.

If you are not clear on what you should and should not say on the telephone, stand back for a moment and listen to what the caller is stating. How would a jury view your response? Would a jury consider anything that you say incriminating? So pretend that a jury of your peers is listening to you every time you speak. These are not your friends that you're speaking to, so govern yourself accordingly and think before you speak. You never know when you're being taped. It is that simple.

Let's check our progress:

We have come a long way baby! The yellow pages are distributed, the website is on the first page with pertinent keywords in the top three search engines, we have a good idea how to answer phones, and we have the independent contractor agreement ready. Our agency is almost rolling here, except we have no escorts. We must learn a few things about the ladies that work for escort agencies, and then we will discuss how to collect the money – the entire reason for getting into this business to begin with.

Chapter Eleven – The Escorts

One thing here is certain, and that is the fact that we cannot run an escort business without escorts. Interacting with the escorts is really not that complicated if you have experience dealing with people. Escorts are people, and like you, their goal is to make plenty of money. Understand that no one goes into the escort business purely for fun; you didn't and neither are the escorts. Once you find several dependable escorts the daily business will run smoothly.

You will receive a flood of calls from escorts as soon as the yellow pages are distributed because you are new in town, and many have had troubles with other services. You never want to ask another service about an escort that's seeking work. It is unlikely that the other service would be honest with you, and perhaps the escort needs a fresh start. You will also start receiving calls from escorts that viewed your website, as soon as the site is listed in *Maps* and in the first or second page of results in *Google*. In the beginning it's a good idea to place an ad in the "Adult Gigs" category of *Craig's List*, and you may want to do this periodically throughout this venture.

When I first opened in Orlando, before the yellow pages were fully distributed, I went to men's clubs, mainly *Club Juana*, paid for dances, and wrapped a business card in the tip. At one point I had four or five dancers moonlighting as escorts, but they started arguing about calls and money at work, a manager caught wind of it, and all of the dancers were warned that if they were discovered working as escorts, they would be fired from the club. Two of the dancers chose my agency over the club, and one was a feature entertainer, Jade. Club managers despise escort services, so use caution with this.

By the time the yellow pages are fully distributed you will hear from plenty of escorts. What do you say when an escort calls looking for work? Well, you have to decide on the type of ladies you want to work with, and the ages of the escorts. I preferred escorts 28 and older, but then this could lose you a lot of calls, and I really wouldn't advise it if you can deal with 21 and over. I'd never advise anyone to work with the 18, 19, and 20 year-olds – it's just too much trouble. At that age they're trying to make money in-between parties and you really want escorts that take this seriously.

If you are middle-aged as I am, you will find that working with the 18 to 21 crowd is more trouble than it's worth, regardless of the fact that it is absolutely legal. These are the escorts that you will have to chase-down to collect from and any schedule of availability is close to worthless. You will quickly learn that the best escorts at any agency are over 30. The problem is that some of the callers are unaware of this fact. For this reason we will set the age requirement as over 21 years.

One other thing that I did differently than most escort agencies is require that escorts have experience, even if it was experience as a dancer in a men's club. The reason for this is that I do not train anyone. It's not my thing as it requires answering questions constantly about the simplest situations, like calling and checking-in upon arrival or how to call a client. Often inexperienced escorts do not know how to talk to men on a phone, so never have one calling the clients as chances are good that he will cancel. The best description of the job that I could give an inexperienced escort is to tell her that she is an actress and this is her stage.

I knew another agency owner that only worked with inexperienced escorts. Crystal wanted nothing to do with anyone that had worked as an escort previously. She liked to train the escorts to do things her way, and she felt that the experienced escorts were all thieves. Often she called me with appointments and we would split the fee as she had no escorts available, and few ladies at my service could tolerate her. Usually they would refuse to tolerate her, and had no interest in accepting the appointment if they had to speak to her, even on a phone. Sometimes I wouldn't tell them where the call came from, but Crystal would call the client while the escort was there. She tried to convince escorts to work for her more than once this way, but in each case I heard about it instead. Crystal managed to alienate almost every escort that she encountered. Don't be like Crystal.

In the first few months of business, I would advise you to only work with experienced escorts, otherwise it would be somewhat like the blind leading the blind. After a few months you can always revisit the decision and change your policy. I also advise you to give the escorts, or potential escorts, the idea that you have had escort businesses for years and just recently made the move to open in X city. If they think you are naïve, chances are good that many will take advantage. Just remember that the escorts are people and it's not that complicated. Whatever you do, never deal with an escort's driver if she has one. Her driver is her problem and you only speak to the escort.

What do I say to an escort seeking work?

When escorts call your number seeking work you should first clarify where they found your number. You want to know if the escort is looking through the yellow pages or found you in an online directory or viewed your website. Talk to everyone that calls as just about anyone is worth a minute of your time. The usual question is: "Are you hiring?" The answer will always be that yes, you do need a couple additional escorts. The reasoning is that you might find someone that is great to work with. Here is a list of questions you would want to ask on the phone before you go out and meet any potential escort:

1. Have you ever worked as an escort before? In Miami? Where?

You want to have an idea if this potential escort has really ever worked as an escort; some state that they have because they're desperate and since you are not going to train escorts, you do not need the problem. Ask her questions about where she worked and why she decided to call your ad. Something went wrong or she wouldn't be calling you. Realize that many agencies run lousy operations. Also realize that she will probably not tell you the truth. The answer only matters in relation to establishing that she has in fact worked as an escort before.

2. What hours/days are you available? Are there specific nights that you are unable to work?

This question will allow you to find out more about the person calling. Usually you will have all of these questions answered by asking this two-part question. Does she have a night job? Does she have a husband or boyfriend and intend to works as an escort behind their back? Is she going to school (college)? Does she have children? Does she have a babysitter problem or is the situation under control?

This really helps you to get to know her and decide if it's worth it to you to meet with her. If she answers that she can never work after 9pm, it's unlikely that you'll want to bother, but watch out for the escorts that answer that their availability is 24/7 – this is rarely true. Make the 24/7 escort call on when she's available, and call off when she's not; otherwise you will book her and she won't answer and will later offer some excuse why she couldn't answer. You are seeking a realistic answer of her hours. Realistic is her stating that she can't work until 9m, but will be available until 5am, just about any night.

3. Please give me a basic description. You are seeking: age; height; weight; approximate measurements; hair color and length. Add: Can you email me a full length photo? (nothing nude or crude and preferably with her wearing a dress)

You do need escorts that are height/weight proportionate. You do not need any "big beautiful women" because you will never be able to send one to a call. I am not in great shape, but then I am not working as an escort either. The men that call (99%) want someone in great shape or slender. Sorry, but it is how it is, and there isn't a thing that you can do about it, so do not waste your time meeting with big escorts. To have an escort or two that is describable as "voluptuous" is a good idea, but not when she is nearing 200 lbs; be careful with this or you will lose your clients quickly. Age should be over 21, mainly because women that are over 21 have more of an idea of what they want to do in life. Other than this factor, you want escorts in a variety of ages. In so far as height is concerned, short, medium, or tall is good. You want escorts of all heights, varying nationalities, and with a variety of hair colors. The most requested description is that of *Barbie*. Go figure.

4. Where do you live?

You are not seeking her address. You are looking for an area when you ask this question; a section of Miami, such as Miami Beach, South Beach, the Grove, Coral Gables, North Miami etc.... If she is in Fort Lauderdale you do not want to waste your time meeting with her because you are not currently operating in Lauderdale, besides, there are plenty of services in Lauderdale for her to call.

You do want to have escorts in different areas of Miami.

This is about all that you need for an initial phone conversation that is actually a mini-interview. After speaking with her, if you are interested, you will want to schedule an appointment that evening; usually 7pm to 9m is normal. If she puts you off and wants to make it the following day, you need to tell her to call you the following day and you'll see what your schedule looks like. Never set interviews for another day. Try to schedule a couple of interviews at a time, within 30 minutes of each other. It's best to meet for coffee at *Starbucks* or *Dunkin Donuts*. This way you can sit at a table and have a ten to fifteen minute conversation. Always schedule the interviews at a location that's convenient to you. Ask her to dress as she would dress if going to a call in a hotel downtown. Talk about dress requirements and the need to blend-in in any environment. You will see if she understood when you meet her.

Make sure that you ask her if she has a driver's license or a state ID at the end of the conversation, if you are scheduling an interview. Tell her to bring it as you will need to see it.

Dress Requirements

There is no "one size fits all" explanation in relation to dress requirements. The idea is for the escort to blend-in for the specific location that she is dispatched to. If the escort is going to a South Beach hotel she should be dressed according to the time of day or night, but always dressed well, as everyone else will be. If the escort is going to a downtown hotel, say the *Marriott*, again the time of day is important. She shouldn't look like she's ready to go out for the night at 5pm. She should look like any guest in the hotel at the hour that she is going there. An escort going to the *Marriott* downtown will dress differently than an escort going to a South Beach hotel. Drive around, get out, and see how people dress in different locations. One atmosphere is party and the other is business.

Make-up is a must. If you encounter an escort that doesn't wear make-up, just move-on. Men that call escorts are looking for ladies that know how to apply make-up and dress. For hopefully obvious reasons, perfume is never a good idea. Some perfumes are stronger than others and it's just best to have a "no perfume" policy.

The only time that jeans are acceptable is when the escort is going somewhere that most people are wearing jeans, and this will be a rare occasion. I used to make it a point to meet an escort as she leaves a hotel, say in the parking-lot, and always caught the jeans fan. I would give a couple of warnings, and that was it. I once discovered an escort coming out of a call in a sweat-suit! I collected my money, let her make-up excuses, left, and never called her again. There is no excuse for an escort wearing such attire to a call. No one wants to pay $400 an hour for an escort in a sweat-suit. You do not want hotel personnel, such as bellmen, valets, concierges, or the front desk people to think that your agency sends out shabbily dressed escorts.

Nails are important too. They shouldn't be too long and they should be fresh and clean looking, like a French manicure. No client wants an escort that has the nails and hands of a dishwasher. It should go without saying, but the shoes should fit the outfit; in other words, sneakers do not go with anything that she is supposed to be wearing.

You will find that the great majority of experienced escorts know how to dress as they want to blend-in and not stand-out in the crowd. The escorts should never be recognizable as escorts.

The Interview

You want to bring a notepad so that you can write down the escort's description as you view her. You should have the notes from her initial phone-call to you. This should be a ten to fifteen minute interview and no longer. Do not get personal with the escort and ask answers to personal questions. In the same respect, do not offer any personal information about yourself. Remember – you are your alias and created persona.

1. First ask for her ID. If she doesn't have an ID, no matter what excuse she offers, get up and leave. Do not say one more word to her. If she has her ID and she is one and the same as the photo, and she's over 21 as she stated on the telephone, continue with the conversation. If she told you that she was 25 years old and she's obviously 40+, let her know that you had asked for her real description for reason, you can sign her on, but will never send her out as being 25 years.

2. Pull out your independent contractor agreement (from Chapter Eight) and place it in front of her. Always carry several extra contracts in your briefcase. Tell her that she would be an independent contractor and not an employee. Tell her to read it and wait while she does so. If she is in agreement she should sign the contract and you will, with her ID in hand, write down her birth date, expiration of ID date, address on the ID, and the ID or driver's license number. You must know the identity of the person that you are dealing with. Don't forget to hand her the ID back. Inform the new escort that an agency representative will sign the agreement and you'll give her a copy in a few days when you collect from her.

3. Stress an important rule to the new escort: She should always answer and be available when she has called-on. If she has called available, you call her for a booking, and she doesn't answer and you must re-book the call, you will probably not call her again. Stress that she makes her own schedule and calls on and calls off, and she must meet her own schedule. You chance losing the call if you must call the client back, and you're here to make money, not lose it.

4. Check that she is dressed appropriately as you instructed. If she is dressed for a downtown hotel call as she should be, let her know that you appreciate that she listened and explain why it's important to blend-in. If she is not dressed as instructed, then ask why. Not many excuses could be acceptable if she is

really interested in working with your agency. Do warn her that this won't be acceptable on your calls, but don't say another word about it. You will find out if she was listening soon enough.

I once met with a woman that showed at the interview in a short tennis outfit. I informed her that this could never be acceptable on a call, and she looked at me and stated: "Look at you. You're wearing jeans." I laughed and responded that I didn't go to the calls, and I walked away. End of meeting.

5. Inform the new escort that for a while, a month or maybe more, someone from the agency will meet her to collect right after a call, but that you will not take her out of her way as you have for the interview. She will be met close to the call and the booking agent will let her know specifically where when she checks out of the call, or you might decide to meet her in the hotel parking lot if it's a hotel call. She should be told to never spend your fees and that you earn your fees when she earns hers.

6. Ask her for her schedule from this moment through the coming week. Inform her that you still expect her to call and say that she is available. Let the escort know that if she needs to call off due to some problem, emergency, or whatever, to do that, but to never leave you thinking that she's on if she's not.

7. Explain your process to her. Let her know that she will usually be able to speak to the client before going to the call; however, until you are comfortable with her calling on her own, it will be a three-way call. Let her know that on occasion you will just send her without her calling.

8. The escort must provide you with a few photos so that you can select one for the website. It will be hard to send her out if you do not have a photo. She should email the photos to you. In the photos she should be wearing a sexy dress. Do not accept or post nude or crude photos.

9. Ask the new escort if she has any questions. She probably won't if you covered everything here and she is an experienced escort.

Remember at the end of the last chapter, in the "important notes" section, how you speak to callers on the phone? This is the same way you speak with this new escort for as long as you know her. If she states anything illegal, or even compromising, you must walk away. This goes for the interview or any other time, on the phone or in-person. Think about how it will sound to a jury of your peers before you say it or acknowledge it.

All of this should take no more than 15 minutes; if it does, you are talking too much or letting her talk too much. When you conclude the interview let the person answering the phone know that the escort will be calling available. If you are answering the phone this is not necessary, of course. Do not forget to sign, or have your partner sign, the agreement and return a copy to the escort after she has completed a few calls. If she is not going to be working with you for one reason or another, you do not need her walking around with a copy of your agreement, so do wait a week or so. And then you move-on to the next interview.

Placing an ad on *Craig's List*

You do not want to wait for escorts to call your ads to begin with. In the very beginning, you should post an ad on *Craig's List* in the "Adult Gigs" category every three days. Specifically, this is the "Gigs" category in the "Adult" section. The ad must be placed on the Miami board – do not place ads in cities everywhere or you'll be flagged to oblivion. Even if you think that you have enough escorts still do this. There is an initial weeding-out period and you will not want to work with many of the escorts that seemed wonderful when you interviewed them. This is the early part of your business and you do not want to be without escorts when you have calls. It's better to have too many than too few as you can always tell an escort that you had no calls that fit her description. Never tell one escort about another escort's calls. Offer as little information as possible when speaking to anyone in this business. Here is an example ad for *Craig's List*:

ESCORT AGENCY HIRING!!! (Miami)

We are an upscale, fully licensed, and established agency in Miami. We need a few more experienced escorts that can be available late night.

Requirements:

Must be over 21 years of age. No exceptions.
Must have a valid driver's license or state ID
Must have experience as an escort
Must have late night availability
Must have your own transportation or someone to drive you. We do not drive you.

If this fits you and you want more information, please include the following in your response:

Your name and the area that you live in
A basic photo – no nudity please
A telephone number that we can reach you on

I will contact you within a few hours.

That is all that you want in the ad. Do not place a telephone number in it. You can use a Yahoo email in the ad if you like, but do not identify your agency names or anything else about your business in the ad. Make sure that you check email for that account frequently when running an ad. You will not bother to respond to anyone that doesn't provide a basic photo and a telephone number. Don't email via reply to ask as you've already asked in the ad. This is basic and you can change anything that's important to you, but remember that potential escorts do not read through a bunch of text anymore than potential clients do. Depending on the escorts that respond, you might tell them about the $200 agency, or you might tell them about the $400 agency when you call their number. Do not tell anyone about both.

Once you meet with an escort you'll know if she fits the higher-priced agency or the lower-priced one. This should give you an easy start with plenty of available escorts. Usually the better escorts will find you via your website, and it should be findable and functional before the yellow pages are actually distributed.

I really do not want to discuss this topic to death because I would like to assume that you have some clue how to speak with people, and the escorts are people. Shortly after I was given the booking job in Miami many years ago, I had to run everything and find escorts too. I had no book, but it's really not that complicated. Just remember all that I have already discussed up to this point in the book. There is one very important topic that I haven't discussed, and that is the thieves. It is that type of business and the thieves will steal every dollar that you let them steal.

The Variety of Thieves

There are different types of thieves that you must look out for in the escort business. The worst, at least to me, is the escort that steals the call point-blank by telling you that the client cancelled or never checks-in and keeps all of the money. This type of thief will probably not call you again because she knows that you know. There's not much that you can do about her, except make her go through the interview process and drive across town to meet you – this eliminates many that want to "start now" and grab a call. You will put a glitch in her plans if you do not give her the client's telephone number and simply tell the client that she's on her way and should arrive in about 45 minutes. You can also three-way the call to the client and remain silent, and if you hear him offer a telephone number, click-off the three-way and call him back. There are clients that try to get the escort to go around the agency, though this does not occur frequently. You will drive towards the call when she does so that you know if she arrives and when. Her car may not be in a driveway and she may be dropped off, so you must watch from nearby if you are at all suspicious. At most she should only be able to steal the one call. Most escorts are not that stupid and do not ruin you and your many possible agencies over one fee. The escort has no real idea how many services you have.

The more prevalent thief in the escort business is the one that passes out her telephone number to all of the clients. It's not so easy to catch her. You will know within a month or so, but that's too many stolen clients. You will have to check on her by calling the client after she checks out to ask him if everything was okay. Really listen to him. If no one wants to see this escort again when you've sent her to plenty of locals, you know something is wrong, especially if the client didn't complain about her. When a client doesn't complain, yet he doesn't want to see an escort again, there's usually a reason, and that reason is usually that he can call her on his own and doesn't need you. For all you know, she might be starting her own private agency with your clients. If he was a regular caller and he suddenly stops calling, she may be sending her friends to him. Look to see if she is keeping the schedule that she provides you, and if not, wonder why. No one really disappears for two hours every other night unless they have something else going.

Another type of thief is the escort that checks out from a call, meets you to pay your fee, lets you know that she's tired or sick or whatever, and then returns to the call for more hours. She is relatively easy to catch. I used to drive away after collecting as if I was clueless, and then go search a hotel parking lot for her car. If I found her car, I would place a business card on the windshield wiper with a note on the back to call me. When she called the following day, I'd tell her that she couldn't be on again until I received four hours in fees ($100 x 4 = $400). She could argue till she was blue in the face that she forgot something and had to return or she only collected one additional hour, but I couldn't care less. Her deceit cost her four hours. If the call was at a residence, I'd double-back after I met her and watch for a bit. If her car was there I'd leave the card, and if she was dropped off I would call her phone and leave a message. Either way, she didn't work again until I was paid. I do not care what she had to say about her return because there is no valid reason to return to a client's location without telling the service.

Until you get to know the escorts that you're working with, you will need to do some detective work. That is how it is. Confronting the escort in person is never a good idea. Either she will pay you or she won't, but at least you did get your fee for one hour, and it isn't so hard to part ways with her. If she does pay you it will be necessary to watch her for a while as she leaves your calls. You might want to charge her a higher fee because she's forced you to play babysitter.

All of these situations are why you need a partner or to hire a driver for errands and collections. My driver would watch and call me with a run-down, and he was gay so these thieving escorts couldn't try to pull the wool over his eyes by acting like they wanted to date him. This is certainly not beyond a thieving escort.

At the same time I must warn you that if your partner is a man, you will need to watch for favoritism towards a specific escort. If it's something that you notice, wonder what is going on. If you are a man, do not do it. They will eat you alive. This reminds me of Richard, an escort service owner that I knew many years ago in Miami. Richard could not keep his hands to himself, and to get more calls an escort might make him believe that she was interested in him. The last pair of escorts that did this did have sex with him to get more calls, but they also later set him up. He was arrested for a list of charges and then pled to racketeering.

The escorts will never be interested in you because they like you. They are there to make money. Do not forget this. I have had escorts try this crap with me, believe it or not, and female escorts at that. I do not care what you perceive the situation to be, just don't go there. A story to make my point:

At one point I knew this escort service owner that used the alias of Bambi. Bambi also sent out male escorts (I did not). Somehow she ended-up seeing a male escort that worked for her business. This guy was good – he eventually talked her into allowing him to move in to her house. She thought it was love, but all he had on his mind was lots of money. He didn't just take her for a financial ride, but when the money became less and less because of Orlando's MBI and the credit card sting operation that Bambi was caught in, he started the blackmail game with her. As soon as he moved in, he started copying her client lists, so he really had all the damning information that could put Bambi away in a prison for a decade. He threatened to take all of the information to the MBI if she didn't pay him large sums of money on a regular basis, like $20K a month. Bambi was scared, didn't know what to do, and allowed him to tell her that the only way to get that kind of money with the MBI all over Orlando services was to work at brothels in Nevada. That is what Bambi did for a while until she became fed-up and there was no longer much to worry about legally. This is why I never mixed business with pleasure.

The escorts, male or female, can be treacherous. Treat it as a business and not as your playground. When you're finished with it all in three years then you can go play elsewhere. Do not start a fine system with the escorts as that will only bring resentment and theft. You will meet some nice escorts that do not seek to steal and beat you at every corner. After a while it will be easy to recognize those escorts as clients will call back and request to see them again and they will never spend your fees. They are not the game-players and they are only in the business to take their own share. It will be easy to tell the difference, just as it is with people in all types of business.

Important Notes

It is important to state that confronting an escort is rarely a good idea. When you back a person into a corner, they will often claw their way out, so don't put yourself in the position to begin with. That's why I would just leave a business card on the car or a message on a phone. I always figured that it was a small loss and she was replaceable if she didn't come to me and pay what she owed for her theft. When she finds that card or receives your message she will call, if your agency is of any value whatsoever to her, or if she doesn't know who you know and who you don't know. For all she knows you could blacklist her and she would be unable to work in Miami again. She doesn't know that you do not speak to other agency owners, so don't tell her. Confrontation is just not a good idea. When you stop giving an escort calls, you just put her on a backburner and don't call her. Let her call in for as long as she wants. It's easy to say, "Okay, I'll call you if I get anything, but it's really dead." Eventually she will get the picture without you informing her of her status. The reality is that she will also know why.

Watch out for drug users. If you cannot tell when you first meet an escort, you will know within a month. These escorts are always thieves in one way or another and will only cause problems. You will encounter this type with your lower-priced service. Also listen for an intoxicated escort – if she has been drinking, she shouldn't be driving. If you need to pick her up at the call and drive her home, then that is what you do, but don't let her drive drunk. Of course this depends how long she was at the call, I mean if it can be cured with a few cups of coffee at *Denny's* then just go there for breakfast with her. Most escorts know not to get drunk at a client's place, but sometimes a drink will intoxicate. Just listen and keep your eyes open. I once had an escort so intoxicated by the conclusion of a four-hour call that the client called me begging me to get her out of there. All they did was get drunk for four hours (both of them). I dealt with it. Just take it step by step. It is a learning experience for anyone.

Do not toss aside what you have read in this book. I spent many years in the escort business and learned the hard way more than once. You will meet some nice people also, so don't let what I've stated scare you away. Sometimes you will be social with the escorts, or even the clients, and that is normal. This is a social business and most clients call because they're bored or lonely. Be flexible but cautious at the same time. Most important, always remember that the jury of your peers could be listening to your every word so watch what you say to anyone that you encounter, on the phone or in person.

Chapter Twelve – Collecting Your Money

Collecting your money may sound like a non-issue to you, but I consider it important enough for a short chapter. You have already read some thoughts on the topic, though nothing in-depth. My first rule is never loan the escorts money because it's unlikely that you will ever see it again, and you're not a bank anyway. I never borrowed money and never loaned money with the escort business. Well, that is not exactly true, but the time I did loan money I never saw it again. What seemed like an intelligent move and a nice thing to do was just dumb. People will think that you are filthy rich and they will ask. That is one reason that you are better off playing the lowly employee of the company role. Do not oblige the wannabe borrowers. You don't need friends that want money. Friends like this are a dime a dozen.

When an escort first starts working with your business you will need to collect after every call, but as time goes on, you'll start to be lax, perhaps intending to collect after the next call, but in the escort business anything can happen and there may not be a next call for the particular escort. You always want to collect your money if it is at all possible, and it should be doable as it's why you're in the business to begin with. Much of your night, or your partner's or driver's, will be spent running around collecting money.

I used to use my business checking account for this purpose frequently. I would give escorts that I knew and trusted deposit slips and they would deposit the following business day. If I didn't see the money in the account, which happened sometimes, I'd call the escort and ask why. Sometimes there was an honest explanation, so I'd let it go, but other times I would ask the escort to meet me with my fees. This really worked for me; however, in the court case that followed my arrest I received 3 years of copies of deposit slips along with the 3 years of copies of checks written in discovery. This is all public information and viewable by anyone, except that in my case the file disappeared and then the recreated file disappeared. It was a special case indeed. All I did was add to the state's volume of paperwork – nothing illegal there, mind you, but nevertheless more paper crap.

When I filed a civil rights suit after my acquittal one of the reasons the federal judge stated for dismissing my suit was that an escort deposited money into my business bank account, and it was in fact my business bank account. When the particular escort was arrested at a call, the MBI found a deposit receipt in her purse. It was a big find for the MBI. Personally, I would have considered it to be more of an issue if I didn't have a business account. I considered the entire mention of it to be ridiculous and certainly not a valid reason to dismiss my suit. I think that any attorney would agree with me. Regardless, these people didn't like my perfectly legal structure because this happened in Orlando. Just pass on the deposit slip fee payment and skip the paperwork. I considered it to be like discussing the price of tea in China: absolutely immaterial.

When you collect your fees in person, always listen to what the escort is saying. You never know, she might have been arrested, and law enforcement might be feeding her words that would incriminate you. If in doubt, walk away without a word. It is not worth any discussion whatsoever. The chance of this happening is slim, but always be aware.

Just collect the fees after the calls if at all possible. With escorts that you know well enough to trust a day or two, you can meet at *Starbucks* for coffee the following evening. I say this because a call may not conclude until 6am, 7am, or later, and the last thing that you'll feel like doing is running across Miami in morning traffic if the escort is trustworthy anyway.

Although this should go without saying here, I'll say it: Your fees should be in cash. You will not accept any form of payment other than cash, from clients or escorts. Do not accept a check from an escort anymore than you would from a client. Sometimes you'll end-up with foreign money, hopefully

Euros, and that is fine as long as you check the exchange rate and calculate any possible fee. Always accept Euros, British Pound Sterling, or Canadian Dollars from clients. Any other currency requires an evaluation at the time, by you of course.

Go forth with my best wishes and make lots of money to collect. The escort business is what you make it.

About the Author

I first answered escort service telephone lines in Miami, back in 1984. The business belonged to Kim, and I have no clue what ever happened to her after I relocated west in 1987. My three years of experience in Miami back in the 1980s answering escort service telephone lines prompted the idea to open my own agency in Orlando in 1992. That agency was in business until the end of September of 2001 when I closed it. My research for three books landed me back in the world of escort services, though not with the goal of running a business or profiting from it, but in developing up to date information. At this point in my life my only goal is to live long enough to finish the next book, and it looks as if I have a chance to accomplish this goal.

During the years that I was in business in Orlando I opened many (more than 20) escort businesses in Florida that I sold as soon as the yellow pages were distributed. I did not start these businesses with the intention of selling and transferring each; however, by the time that directories were published and distributed, plans changed due to unforeseeable situations in my own life or with my Orlando services. I am capable of opening and operating a profitable escort service in just about any location in the US.

About two months after I closed my services in Orlando, the Metropolitan Bureau of Investigation (MBI) arrested me on a list of charges. The two charges that were actually filed by Florida's Office of the Statewide Prosecutor (OSP) are: racketeering; and conspiracy to commit racketeering (RICO). In Florida, each is a first degree felony punished by up to thirty years in a Florida prison. I took the State of Florida to trial and on January 17, 2003, a jury of my peers returned "not guilty" verdicts on both counts after deliberating for under one hour.

I will be the first to admit that the arrest and trial took its toll on me. I believe that it has taken at least ten years from my life. I know that it had effects on me that will always remain. The MBI stole my ability to trust people. I never really was a people person, but by the time the case was over I wanted little to do with anyone outside of my immediate family. In a sense, the case continues to this day – the OSP and the MBI did not take losing lightly, and the former agents and representatives have sought to discredit me on any and all forums. The character attacks have never ceased, and often one of the many that despise me will create stories that serve to discredit my person and character. Yes, I could track down the perpetrator through an IP address and file a libel suit, but as of this point in time, I have chosen not to do so. I may in the future.

Funny, but I haven't heard a word from their direction since *Memoirs of an Accused Madam: The War on Adult Business in Orlando* was published; funny except that I know they're up to something and will reveal it when they're ready. I will always be tracked in America. There is no peace for me in this country and I cannot leave as my mother is older and not in the best of health. Indeed, they are sore losers. Obviously, operating an escort service and making money at it is never possible for me again. It is possible for anyone not under a magnifying glass. I would never suggest opening an escort business in Orlando though. Orlando is different.

Today I reside in Orlando and in Cape Canaveral – there is a forty-five mile distance between these two areas and I'm back and forth frequently. When the case was over I did finish my bachelor's degree – a B.A. concentrating on social and economic history from the State University of New York (SUNY). I then began graduate studies in history; however, decided that the pursuit was not in my best interest and eventually quit before earning the master's degree. I appreciate my education, but will never be able to use it to find employment because of the background checks. Public records reveal my arrest and fail to note my acquittal by jury. I have never been convicted of anything except a minor traffic infraction.

You are receiving the benefit of my 13 years of experience in the escort business for the low price of this book, and the 13 years doesn't include several years of knowledge developed from the arrest, case, and trial that resulted in my acquittal by jury. If you are going to read advice and operational plans in relation to the escort business, don't you want that advice to come from the one escort service owner in this country that beat racketeering and conspiracy charges?

Author's Information

If you have any question that I have left unanswered, feel free to contact me through email or the U.S. mail. I will promptly respond. If you require a special consultation, something that cannot be answered in an email or is more than a few questions, I do charge a consultation fee. I will quote the charge on a case-by-case basis, and the consultation would probably be over the telephone. The fee would be payable through PayPal.

vlgallas@gmail.com

or

Vicky Gallas
8501 Astronaut Blvd. Suite 5, # 165
Cape Canaveral, FL 32920

If you enjoyed the author's approach to the escort business read *The Accused Madam* blog on Amazon for current news specific to adult business legal prosecutions and escort businesses.

8513827R0

Made in the USA
Lexington, KY
07 February 2011